A POCKET GUIDE TO
HCI AND UX
DESIGN

A POCKET GUIDE TO HCI AND UX DESIGN

DR. ANIRBAN CHOWDHURY

Associate Professor & Head
User Experience & Interaction Design
School of Design (SoD),
University of Petroleum and Energy Studies (UPES)
Dehradun-248007, Uttarakhand, India

PARTRIDGE

To order additional copies of this book, contact
Partridge India
000 800 919 0634 (Call Free)
+91 000 80091 90634 (Outside India)
orders.india@partridgepublishing.com

www.partridgepublishing.com/india

CONTENTS

ACKNOWLEDGEMENT

I want to sincerely thanks to my Mother and Wife for constant support and motivating me to write this book. I want to acknowledge to my students – Ms. Prachi Karkun, Mr. Sayantan Chaudhuri, Ms. Richa Shevde, Ms. Devyani Shirole and others for sharing their illustrations for this book. I want to show my sincere gratitude to Mr. Sridhar Dhulipala (UX-consultant), Mr. Sachin Patil (Microsoft, India), Mr. Hemant Suthar (Co- founder Fractal ink, India) for providing valuable insights on this book and agreed to publish their interviews in this book.

Messages from an Industry Expert

Mr. Sridhar Dhulipala
Product and UX consultant
Total Experience in the Field (in Years): 25

According to publicly available data, the market for UX design services is expected to be upwards of USD 11 billion by 2022. This assumes a compounded annual growth rate of over 15%. I see this as riding on the back of a larger trend i.e. Digital transformation and adoption that all sectors are seeing, which ranges from fintech to agriculture. UX services share of this market is expected to be 3-4% in overall value terms of what is seen as USD 450 billion digital transformation market. In 2001-2, when I setup the UX competency group at Infosys, as a companywide, horizontal service, we were a studio of two dozen designers. Post 2010, with the adoption of digital and cloud, growth of smartphones, shift to agile methodologies, and superior tools for designer-developer collaboration there is a significant demand, which at over 15% growth is higher than top IT initiatives.

In India, the demand is not limited to large services IT companies such as Accenture, TCS, IBM, Infosys, and others but a lot of startups, from unicorns to seed funded.

Digital India is a serious initiative from Government of India with its ambitious goal of USD 1 Trillion digital economy by 2025. Government has been very rapid at adoption and rolling out of digital services across ministries. At a policy level central ministry are committed to principles of universal design, accessibility and usability. In my own personal interactions with top Government officials, there is a clear emphasis on good, usable design. Government organizations are working with institutions like NID, NIFT and IITs to achieve these objectives. They also work with empanelled private organizations to deliver good design in their initiatives. According to apps.nic.in there are over 61 citizen facing apps with popular apps like Bhim, IRCTC, Mygov, Digilocker, mpassport, 112app, Umang and several others, there is a recognition that apps need to be well designed. Demand for UX in Governments both central and rest is strong.

Learning to Design is largely experiential as a skill, where learning comes from doing. Also, design draws on knowledge from several disciplines such as psychology, ergonomics, art and aesthetics, craft, science, engineering, management, marketing, so on. Each of these disciplines is relevant to various aspects of design activities ranging from design research, ideation, prototyping, testing so on. Your proposed book will be useful for design students and practitioners who need a ready reference to help navigate their learning. A book such as this covers several of these aspects and definitely adds to the growing repository of design literature. Design process and methodologies are increasingly important in this age of close and active collaboration. Design before the rise of consumer tech and demand for good UX used to be a black-box activity that was not well understood, or was commonly perceived as merely about making interfaces 'look good.' This book by outlining current popular practices, processes and terminologies will help students and practitioners to better integrate into multi-disciplinary project teams and perform more efficiently.

When compared to other disciplines such as economics, medicine, sciences, mathematics, social sciences, management, so on design has fewer books available as a choice. Often a lot of design books celebrate the aesthetic aspects that end up as light reading. For serious practitioners and students who will turn into design professionals, a serious, in-depth book is always necessary. This category is small and hence there is an opportunity for more relevant literature. Further, given rapid changes in our markets, where adoption of digital technologies, artificial intelligence, agile process, are being witnessed, a book that accounts for these challenges is very important. Design like every other profession is successfully adapting to digital. While designers continue to remain attached to pencil and paper tools, they prefer digital tools in projects to create, share, communicate. This book covers several of these contemporary issues and hence should be well received.

Messages from an Industry Expert

Mr. Sachin Patil
Principal Design Manager
Microsoft, India.

It is quite understandably increasing. Especially in IT product world, there are more specialisations expected off late with HCI research skills separate and design specialisations like interaction and visuals.

This book definitely looks like good content to help learners establish the baseline. Somewhere just the clarifications around terms like users, customers, research, and design may be needed. May be further bifurcating difference in academic research and industry's perception on pragmatic research.

It definitely will, especially with given context chapters like "Elementary ideas on AR, VR and XR based interfaces", "Tangible interfaces" and AI BOT experiences are of tremendous value.

Industry practices have evolved from 'money ball' strategies to 'system thinking' recently and then with the backdrop of tech evolutions, it is quintessential to consider AR, VR, XR and of course AI, BOT interactions for making it relevant. There is this weird aspect of phygital where physical experiences are mixed with digital world. This book may be able to establish the baseline for those speculative design considerations.

Personally, I would have loved to have this book much earlier. Somewhere the perceptions around UX are quite different in different markets. This book surely will add value to all those who are looking for single source of information around UX.

Messages from an Industry Expert

Mr. Hemant Suthar
Co- founder,
Fractal ink, India.

Just like architects are needed for Building, Construction and Planning, UX designers are needed for all digital products. World was slowly transitioning in to a digital and automated one with power of Machine learning and AI, With COVID-19 this process has accelerated and what was a luxury then has now become a necessity. Designers help various industries analyse and understand their ecosystem, come up with insights to show how their products or services connect with customers and identifies the problems that they may not even know about. Designers are geared to find the "unknowns" and in today's times industries cannot do without them.

A Governments role is to provide unbiased and equal opportunity/service to every citizen. From Central government to local Municipal offices, everyone is using digital and mobile tools to improve public service and utilities. Digital transformation of governance is happening across the world. A UX designer provides impactful improvements in customer experience through informed, deep understanding of users. and I see a great demand for them now and in near future.

This book covers the fundamental principles of HCI/ UX design. it goes into a lot of detail and depth on things, which will make it very useful to set the foundation for the learner. It will provide both technical and emotional framework to understand and solve problems. This book has all the essential ingredients you need to understand, from the history, cognitive ergonomics, processes, methods and strategies to future technologies. I think this book will gear up the learner with a rich vocabulary to articulate his ideas clearly.

It will be a great toolkit for academicians as it contains all the essential ingredients and I see it becoming a textbook for teaching HCI/UX design. This book can also help them design curriculum for their students.

From Strategy to wireframes to look and feel, each part should pick up from where the other left and come together in the final form to create a seamless experience for the end user. This book covers both UX process and methods in detail with examples of applications. This will help the learner understand the pros and cons of each method and help them find the right mix for solving their problem. The content of this book is relatable to industry practices, depending on the project timelines and constraints the learner will be in a position to tweak and create a right mix for a given problem.

I see a great market for this book as very few books have been published on this subject from the Indian context and from the perspective of a designer. This will also be a must have reference book in an HCI/UX designers toolkit.

CHAPTER 1

HCI and UX Design on Booming

Key learnings -

- ❖ Definitions of HCI and UX design
- ❖ Scopes of application of knowledge of UX design in various fields
- ❖ Important terminologies and debates related to HCI and UX design
- ❖ Job prospects in industry and government agencies

1. What is HCI and User Experience Design?

Human computer interaction is a scientific discipline which is focused on the interaction between human beings and computers (including mobile devices, tablets, laptops, and any other devices involving computer-like capabilities). The HCI study encompasses multiple disciplines such as computer science, ergonomics/ human factors engineering, electronics and electrical sciences, psychology, design etc. Humanizing computing devices is the key goal in case of any HCI study.

User Experience (UX) Design is a HCI allied discipline. The UX design mainly focuses on human capabilities and satisfaction aspects through study of user behaviour and provides optimal solutions for any kind of problems related to human life in creative and innovative ways. An UX designer generally has skillset to design systems, information architecting, exploration of interaction types and navigation design for various platforms, various kinds of user interface (UI) design, usability testing, service experience design etc. along with user research and data analytics. A basic framework is depicted in **Fig.1.1**. A UX designer can involve themselves in various kinds of solutions such as -

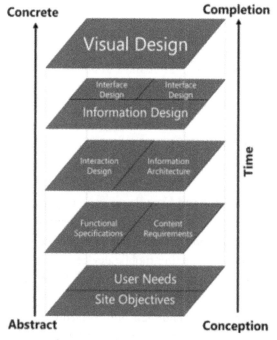

Fig. 1.1 Basic framework for UX design (reproduced the Jesse James Garrett and adapted from Design Thinking Book by DMI).

1. User research and user requirement analysis in any design context
2. Software design and its GUI design (desktop-based apps, mobile apps and web apps etc.)
3. Software based service experience and quality improvements
4. Optimization of interactions and experiences for tangible interactive products
5. Optimization of interactions and experiences of internet of things (IoT)
6. Optimization of interactions and experiences artificial intelligence (AI) based solutions
7. Analysis and visualization of data for improvement of product or service quality
8. Optimization of interactions and experiences of immersive environment (VR, AR, MR etc.) based solutions

Scopes are not limited to above mentioned areas, but many more. Application of HCI and UX design principles are applicable for almost every business. Therefore, the business sense and entrepreneurial mind set of HCI experts or UX designers are essential for them. In academia, HCI has been studied under different Schools of Computer Sciences; whereas, UX and Interaction Design has been studied under many Design Schools across the globe.

Fig. 1.2 Responsibility wise differences between UI and UX designers.

2. Demand of HCI and UX Design Skills in Industry

There is a huge demand for HCI specialists and UX designers in industry. If UX designers are in high demand in the field of design and computer science. Around 70 % of learners of UX and Interaction design get jobs with high salary packages throughout the world among all other jobs. Average packages in HCI/ interaction design/ UX design jobs in India are about INR 6.5 lakhs after successful completion of undergraduation programme (UG) and INR 8.5 Lakhs after postgraduation studies.

3. Important Terminologies and Job Roles

Though, there are terminology wise differences in job roles for UX designers/ HCI experts in industry, they are performing almost similar tasks. Recent debates by industry experts and academicians highlighted the differences between UX and UI design (Please see **Fig. 1.2.**). In this context, it should be considered that UI designers should have clear knowledge about requirements of their target users, without this knowledge user satisfaction/ a good user experience could not be achieved. Many UI design experts (graphic/ visual designers who are playing the roles of UI designers in industry) often confuse or ignore this fact, rather they only focus on visual delightness or aesthetics aspects of graphical user interface (GUI). Further, GUI is not only a kind of user interface, but there are many other kinds of interfaces such as tangible user interfaces, voice user interfaces, other IoT based natural user interfaces (e.g. gesture-based interface) where GUI is less observed. Even, in some cases no GUIs are observed (e.g. Amazon Alexa). Therefore, experts who are working in this field with various job roles in industry need to clear the concept that UX is the integral part for all kinds of interface design. Many academicians and industry experts also feel that UI design is small part of UX design, when UX design is the bigger umbrella (**see Fig. 1.3.**).

Fig. 1.3 Visual spectrum of UI and UX design.

UX designers also need to aim for good experiences at various touch points (e.g. before product/service/ software launch to marketing to post marketing association with target users/ consumers) (Please see **Fig. 1.4**). There are few terminologies like Consumer Experience (CX) and Total User Experience (TUX) are currently floating in the

Industry ecosystem. However, conceptually these are the same. In this context it is important to highlight that the UI design is small part to achieve the overall user experience.

Fig. 1.4. Various touch points and consumer journey.

Bibliography

1. Dix, A., Finlay, J., Abowd, G. D., & Beale, R. (2000). Human-computer interaction. *Harlow ua*.
2. Lockwood, T. (2010). Design thinking: Integrating innovation, customer experience, and brand value. Simon and Schuster.

CHAPTER 2

Cognitive and Affective Human Factors in HCI & UX design

Key learnings -

- ❖ Definitions of human factors
- ❖ Domains of Ergonomics
- ❖ Cognitive Human Factors and its Applications
- ❖ Affective Human Factors and its Applications

1. What is Human Factors/ Ergonomics?

According to International Ergonomics Association (IEA), Human Factors/ Ergonomics is a scientific discipline in which human-machine interaction has been studied considering the surrounding environment. In USA this subject is popular as Human Factors however in UK and India it is more popular as Ergonomics. In Japan, the same subject is well known as human ergology. The term 'Ergonomics' came from two Greek words – 'Ergon' meaning 'work 'and 'Nomos' meaning 'law'. Hence, human factors/

ergonomics also defined as 'laws of work' or 'principles of tasks'. Currently, in UX practice we give emphasis of the task analysis and come up with taskflow-oriented software design.

2. Domains of Ergonomics

Although this discipline is further extended in to various sub-domains, broadly classified into three -

- *Physical Ergonomics* - concerned with human anthropometry, biomechanics and human physiology and its relation to any task
- *Cognitive Ergonomics* - concerned with sensation, perception, attention, memory, emotion, reasoning, information processing, decision making etc. in relation to task and design strategies.
- *Organizational Ergonomics* - concerned with analysis of organizational structure, organization psychology and policies to optimize job satisfaction and job performance.

Among these domains cognitive ergonomics more relates with UX design solutions. However, sometimes physical ergonomics consideration is also important when we talk about the UX of physical space and tangible interactive products.

3. Cognitive Human Factors and its Applications

Cognitive human factors deal with the study of user behaviour to identify user requirements. Many user studies focus on understanding of mental models of user while performing a task. The goal of UX designers to understand the mental model of target users and design the flow of the software so that it matches with users' mental model.

Let us gain some elementary knowledge on cognitive human factors before understanding the human information processing and application of cognitive ergonomics principles.

Sensation – it is the process of conversion of stimuli (present in surrounding environment) into neural form of energies which human brain can sense. Different sensory receptions are helping in conversion of all kinds of stimuli into nerve impulses and these receptors acting like a transducer. Hence, receptors are also known as biological transducers. For instance, rod and cone cells are acting as visual receptors (present in retina of human eyes) and these are responsible for conversion of visual stimuli in to neural impulses which brain can process and understand the presence of visual stimuli. Another example, auditory hair cells (present in human cochlea, part of an auditory system) are responsible for conversion of sound into nerve impulses and thus helping in auditory sensation.

Perception – it the process of interpretation of stimuli based on past experiences. Perceptual process also requires human attention and involves different memories (specially the short-term memory and long-term memory). Colour perception, shape/ form perception, size perception, depth perception and illusions are related to visual perception; whereas, pitch perception, loudness perception and sound localization are related to auditory perception. Tactual (touch) perception is sometime important for understanding the surface quality of objects or products, temperature and pain.

Fig. 2.1. Perception of visual illusion.

Perception matters and it depends on the way you see the world. For instance, if you scan the fig. X from the left you can see there are 4 columns whereas when you scan from the right side, you may see the 3 columns. This figure is also an example of visual illusion (Please see **Fig.2.1**).

Attention – it is the phenomenon when somebody put their focus for some time on the stimuli present in the surrounding world. There are mainly 3 kinds of attention, focused attention, selective attention and divided attention. When humans focus on a particular are of interest in an environment for a glim of time and then shift to another area of interest, known as focused attention. For instance, when we search and try to identify a word from a paragraph of text, our focus shifts from one word to another word during the search of the word of interest. It is known as selective attention when human beings are focusing or concentrating on a particular area of interest. For example, telescopic vision in which we select a particular area of interest and concentrate on it. Divided attention refers to the attention when splits on multiple objects or areas of interest.

Memory – There are three kinds of memory involved in human information processing. These are: 1) Short-term sensory memory (SSTM) involved in signal transduction (e.g. conversion of visual stimuli into neural energy which is conducted as a nerve impulse to human brain; 2) Short-term memory (STM) which act like computer RAM (random access memory) and its mainly involved in memorisation and memory recall process; 3) Long-term memory (LTM) which stores our experiences.

Cognitive Workload (CWL) – it faced by human being when they need to process a bulk amount of information at the same time as STM has limitation. STM can't process a bulk amount of information at the same time as it has storage limitation. Human being needs to put attention to bits and pieces of information and need to process the information as per the capacity of the STM. The CWL is also known as the mental workload which can be measured by a psychometric scale know as NASA-TLX scale (please refer Chapter 4). Most people think CWL is not good, but its not always true. Goodness of CWL depends on the context e.g. if we need to engage gamers with a gaming interface, in that case CWL might be good and gamers are spending longtime with the game within a limit unless its leading to gaming addiction. If the gamer's engagement is too high with the gaming interface due to CWL then very high CWL is bad for gamers.

Reasoning and Decision Making –

Reasoning is very important function in decision making. There are various logics involved in decision making. Based on logics it is possible to categorize reasoning into four types: 1) *Deductive* reasoning is useful for generalizing a statement in the form of rule(s). For instance, if 'X' is equal to 'Y' and 'Y' is equal to 'Z'; then, 'X' must be equal to 'Z'. In specific, iPhone(s) are mobile phones and all mobiles phones are handy and useful. then all iPhone(s) are handy and useful; 2) *Inductive* reasoning is the exercise to make a general rule from a pattern. For example, if ices are melting in 100 different pots in same conditions, and the melting starts when temperature reaches near a temperature of 10° C, then Inductive reasoning leads to the conclusion that melting temperature of ice is 10° C. 3) Abductive reasoning is the exercise of reasoning in which a solo instance leads to a single rule. For example, if the person A steals a diamond, the person A will leave fingerprints on the diamond display case. This king of reasoning helping designers to provide solutions to problems as they analyze the requirements of the target users. 4) *Innoductive* reasoning applies for realization of phenomenon from a class of probable proposed situations to a larger class of possible realizations. For instance, user experience designers need to understand the property/ feature of a user interface which is beneficial for users before incorporation of these interface features into the software application.

Motor Skills and Actions –

Motor skill refers to the level of precision an operator has for a particular error less physical task/ action. Motor skills are depending on motor learning, age, gender etc. For instances, elderly users may be less precisive when clicking on button on mobile screen as they might have neuromuscular decay. The Fitt's law (described in upcoming section) is related to motor skills of the users.

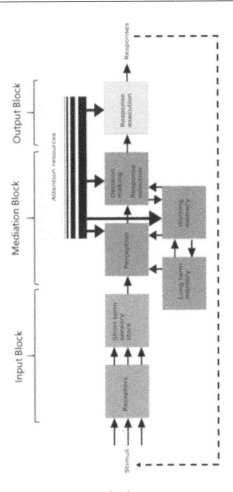

Fig. 2.2 The process of information processing.

3.1. Basic Model of human information Processing

Wickens (2002) has described a basic model of information processing and decision making (Please see **Fig. 2.2**). According to this model, any design solution could be act as a sensory stimulus and processed through either a single or multiple sensory channel with the help of short-term sensory memory.

Then these stimuli are further under go through the perceptual processing for interpretation of stimuli with the help of STM and LTM. The STM is collect the sensory information and recalls the LTM as STM helps to match sensory information with the past experiences (which is stored as LTM). Remember perceptual processing requires attention. Once perceptual processing is complete, reasoning and decision-making takes place. Decision making always require application of different logics in different context. Human being starts execution of response when decision making process is over. Further, the attention is involved in decision-making and execution of various responses.

3.2. Principles of Cognitive Ergonomics
3.2.1. Weber-Fechner Law

The **Weber–Fechner law** refers to two related hypotheses in the field of psychophysics, known as Weber's law and Fechner's law.

Weber law states that "simple differential sensitivity is inversely proportional to the size of the components of the difference; relative differential sensitivity remains the same regardless of size". This means is that the perceived change in stimuli is proportional to the initial stimuli.

Weber's law also incorporates the just-noticeable difference (JND). The JND is the smallest change in stimuli that can be perceived. As stated above, the JND dS is proportional to the initial stimuli intensity S. Mathematically, it can be described as follows:

$$dS = K * S$$

- where S is the reference stimulus and K is a constant
- Fechner's law states that the subjective sensation is proportional to the logarithm of the stimulus intensity
- Hence, $p = k \ln S/S_0$

Perceived loudness/brightness is proportional to logarithm of the actual intensity measured with an accurate nonhuman instrument. Both laws relate to human perception, more specifically the relation between the actual change in a physical stimulus and the perceived change. This includes stimuli to all senses: vision, hearing, taste, touch, and smell. The classic example of JND is the change of size/weight of Cadbury Dairy Milk chocolate (Please see **Fig. 2.3**). They keep changing the size or weight of the chocolate keeping the price as same to gain more profit. However, many consumers ignore such change in weight and purchase the chocolate.

Fig. 2.3. Example of Just Noticeable Difference (JND) where there is a size and weight differences in Cadbury dairy milk but the price is same.

3.2.2. Hick's law

Hick's law states that the time required for making any decision is a function of number of options available to the task context. For example, reaction time is more for searching a menu item from Flipkart than the Amazon as Filipkart menu is not well organized and hierarchy is missing (see **Fig. 2.4**). The opposite situation is true for Amazon menu (see **Fig. 2.5**).

According to this principle the reaction time can be computes as -

$$\mathbf{RT} = a + b \log (\mathbf{n})$$

Where,
RT= Reaction time
a = the total time that is not involved with decision making
b = an empirically derived constant based on the cognitive processing time for each option (value of '*b*' is around 0.155 seconds for humans)
n = number of equally probable alternatives

Fig. 2.4 Organization of menu in flipkart.com.

Fig. 2.5 Organization of menu in amazon.com.

3.2.3. Fitt's law

Fitts' law is used to model the act of pointing, either by physically touching an object with a hand or finger, or virtually, by pointing to an object on a computer display using a pointing device. Equation of Fitts' law for calculation of movement time is as follows:

$$\mathbf{MT} = a + b \times \log_2 \mathbf{ID}$$
$$\mathbf{Or}$$
$$\mathbf{MT} = a + b \times \log_2 (2A/W)$$

In this equation,

MT = Movement time

ID = Index difficulty

a = time which is not involved in cognitive-motor movement.

b = Slope of the linear curve

Fig. 2.6 Importance of distance and area size in Fitt's law.

The movement time is depending on the distance between the button and the initial position of the hand/mouse pointer, whereas, index difficulty is depending on the size of the button (Please see **Fig. 2.6**). According to Fitt's law, the clicking behaviour is depending on position and size of a button on screen. Therefore, UX designer can define the best position of the hamburger menu in the bottom on the mobile screen aligned with the midline of the screen based on the Fitts' law (Please see **Fig. 2.7**)

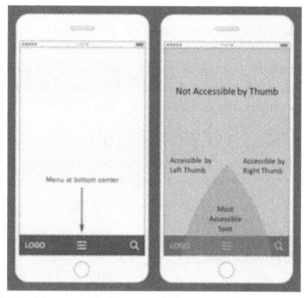

Fig.2.7 Most suitable location of placement of the hamburger menu on mobile screen.

3.2.4. Principles of Conditioning

Classical conditioning is the theory of learning coming under the concept of behaviourism. For most people, the name "Pavlov" rings a bell (pun intended). The Russian physiologist is best known for his work in classical conditioning or stimulus substitution. Pavlov's most famous experiment involved food, a dog and a bell Pavlov's Experiment

- Before conditioning, ringing the bell caused no response from the dog. Placing food in front of the dog, initiated salivation.
- During conditioning, the bell was rung a few seconds before the dog was presented with food.

- After conditioning, the ringing of the bell alone produced salivation

Skinner's work differs from that of his predecessors (classical conditioning), in that he studied operant behavior (voluntary behaviors used in operating on the environment).

Principles of conditioning is applied for many design and strategy instances such as google pay (Please see **Fig. 2.8**).

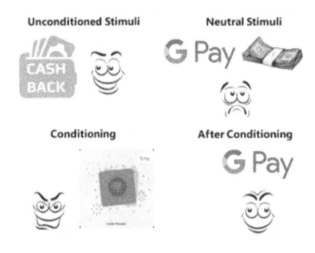

Fig. 2.8 Concept of classical conditioning and G-Pay use.

3.2.5. Principles of Affordance

Gibson intended an affordance to mean "an action possibility available in the environment to an individual, independent of the individual's ability to perceive this possibility" (Gibson 1979. McGrenere and Ho, 2000)

Affordance might be a visual clue to its function and use (Norman 1988) Norman thus defines an affordance as something of both actual and perceived properties. The affordance of a ball is both its round shape, physical material, bouncability, etc.

William Gaver divided affordances into three categories: perceptible, hidden, and false (see **Fig. 2.9**).

A false affordance is an apparent affordance that does not have any real function, meaning that the actor perceives nonexistent possibilities for action. A good example of a false affordance is a dummy button.

A hidden affordance indicates that there are possibilities for action, but these are not perceived by the actor. For example, it is not apparent from looking at a shoe that it could be used to open a wine bottle.

For an affordance to be perceptible, there is information available such that the actor perceives and can then act upon the existing affordance.

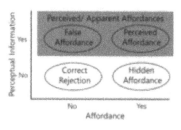

Fig. 2.9 Categorization of affordances.

Table 1. Differences in concepts of affordance.

Gibson's Affordance	Norman's Affordance
Affordances are probable actions in the environment in relation to the action competences of an actor	Affordances are perceived characteristics that may not actually exist or it might be suggestions or clues which are important as to how to use the properties

Affordance is not depending on the actor's experience, knowledge, culture, or ability to perceive	Affordance is depending on the experience, knowledge, or culture of the actor
Existence is binary - an affordance exists or it does not exist.	Affordance either make an action difficult or easy

There are two school of thoughts on affordance theory (Please see **Table 1**). Gibson's affordance theory says that actions in the environment in relation to the action competences of an actor, however, might not depend on past experience of the actor. The example on button design supports the concept of Norman's Affordance theory (**Please see Fig. 2.10**). As he has highlighted in his theory about the relation between the past experience and affordance (**Please see Table 1**).

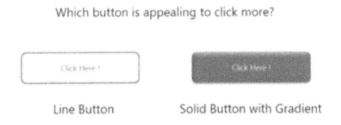

Which button is appealing to click more?

Line Button   Solid Button with Gradient

Fig. 2.10 Solid button with gradient have more affordance might be perceived by Android phone users, but the line button might also have more perceptible affordance among IOS mobile users.

Fig. 2.11 Circumplex model of affect (Adopted from Russell, 1980).

4. Affective Human Factors and its Applications

Affect is the emotion induced action or response by human being; whereas affective state refers to an emotional state of mind. The emotions are feelings associated with the bodily changes. There are six universal emotions according to the great philosopher Charles Darwin. These are fear, anger, disgust, surprise, happiness and sad. Hence, these emotions are predominated across different animals. The affective responses are best explained by the circumplex model by Russell (1980). According to this model, every emotion or affective states are composed of mainly two factors – Arousal and Valance. Arousal is defined as the level of bodily activity; and the valance defines the quality or value of emotion (positive or negative). For instances, anger is a high arousal and negative valance state of humans, happiness is composed of medium arousal and positive valance etc.

Please refer **Fig. 2.11** for understanding the composition of different affective states of human being.

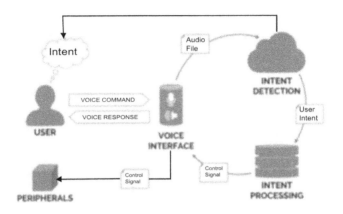

Fig. 2.12 Architecture of a voice recognition system.

The affective state is measured through a subjective rating scale known as Self-Assessment Manikin (SAM) scale. However, UX researchers have also tried to capture different emotions through different methods such as facial electromyography (EMG), pitch and loudness of the voice etc. Following illustration (Please see **Fig. 2.12**) presents the example of voice recognition system for monitoring of affective states based on analysis of pitch and loudness of voice. This kind of system also refers to the application of artificial intelligence (AI).

Patrick W. Jordan has described the pleasure model which is very relevant for UX designers. This model says that there are different user needs like Maslow defined human needs (Please see **Fig. 2.13**). According to Jordan, different user needs are – 1) Functionality, 2) Usability and 3) Pleasure. Users priorities these needs at different levels when they take a purchase or usage related decisions (Please see **Fig. 2.14**). Jordan also highlighted that there are four kinds of pleasures closely affecting the user purchase and usage decisions. These are –

1. Physio-pleasure – related to human touch, comfort etc. of products e.g. light weight and smooth surface of MAC book air gives physio-pleasure to users.
2. Psycho-pleasure – related to aesthetics e.g. GUI (look and feel) of SAMSUNG smartphone interface gives psycho-pleasure to users
3. Socio-pleasure – related to social responsibilities or social communication e.g. people feel social pleasure when they use eco-friendly products
4. Idio-pleasure – related to self-satisfaction and socio-economic status e.g. users shows superiority in social strata when using the costly iPhone leads to idio-pleasure

Fig. 2.13 Maslaw's hierarchy of human needs.

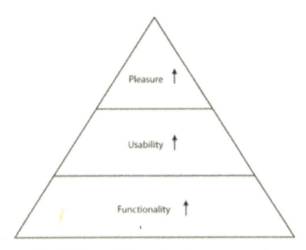

Fig. 2.14 Jordan's hierarchy of consumer needs.

5. Cognitive Human Factors and Accessibility Principles

The accessibility is an important part of usability and it helps to differently abled persons, kids and elderly. Accessibility principles are applicable for universal design approach. Hence it is also known as Universal Design (design for all) principles. Accessibility strategies focuses on –

a. Age
b. Gender
c. Geography, culture and languages
d. Sensory Disabilities (e,g, blindness, deafness and dumbness)
e. Physical Disabilities (Paraplegia, Arm amputee etc.)
f. Mental Disabilities (Amnesia, Dementia, Huntington's Disease, Parkinson's disease etc.) of target users

Hence, UX designers need understand the limitations of different target audiences and their characteristics. Then they should go for user interface design. Accessibility principles include –

1. It should be Perceivable by target users
2. It should be Understandable for target users
3. It should be Operable
4. It should be Robust

Many assistive devices, software and modern physical infrastructures are made based on these principles. For examples, Indian railway implemented ramp in the coach for differently abled in local trains, all express trains have brails for blind users on signages used in toilet, websites of Government of India have accessibility settings on top right corner of the universal menu bar in which users can define sizes of fonts, background colour and languages (Please see **Fig. 2.15**).

One interesting observation is accessibility features of software or product (e.g. voice assistance) are now attractive feature of many upcoming applications or products (e.g. Amazon Alexa) made for physically fit people.

Fig. 2.15 Accessibility setting (highlighted wit rectangle) in the official website of Govt. of India.

Bibliography

1. http://www.dsource.in/course/introduction-cognitive-ergonomics-design

2. Wickens, C. D. (2002). Multiple resources and performance prediction. Theoretical issues in ergonomics science, 3(2), 159-177.

3. https://www.w3.org/TR/?tag=html#w3c_all

4. https://www.w3.org/TR/UNDERSTANDING-WCAG20/intro.html

5. Russell, J. A. (1980). A circumplex model of affect. *Journal of personality and social psychology*, *39*(6), 1161.

6. Bynion, T. M., & Feldner, M. T. (2017). Self-assessment manikin. *Encyclopedia of personality and individual differences*, 1-3.

7. Bynion, T. M., & Feldner, M. T. (2017). Self-assessment manikin. *Encyclopedia of personality and individual differences*, 1-3.

8. e Silva, J. S., Gonçalves, R., Branco, F., Pereira, A., Au-Yong-Oliveira, M., & Martins, J. (2019). Accessible software development: a conceptual model proposal. *Universal Access in the Information Society*, *18*(3), 703-716.

9. Gonçalves, R., Martins, J. L., Au Yong Oliveira, M., Pereira, A., Sousa e Silva, J. S. E., & Branco, F. (2019). Accessible software development: a conceptual model proposal.

***

CHAPTER 3

UX Design Process

Key learnings -

- ❖ Differences between Lean and Agile UX
- ❖ Essential UX design processes
- ❖ Relevance and applications of various UX processes

1. Lean Vs Agile UX Process

In industry, there are broadly two situations –

1) Quick UX solution requirement
2) UX solutions with sufficient time

The lean UX process is generally applied by start-ups and consultancy providing organizations when there is a necessity of a quick deployment of products. However, quick solutions are not always best fit for market as there are limited understanding of target users or market during lean UX process. On the other hand, agile UX process is applicable when solution providers have enough time for UX solutions.

In this context, it was observed that the simple interaction design process is best suited for Lean UX design solutions; whereas, the agile UX process follows the entire usability engineering lifecycle.

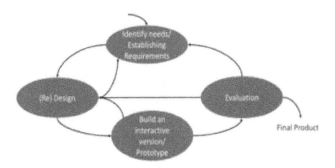

Fig. 3.1 The Simple Interaction Design Process (reproduced from Preece, Sharp, and Rogers, 2014).

2. Simple Interaction Design Process

In this process (Please see **Fig. 3.1**), client or the start-up owner come up with the immediate requirements or needs of a product or software either based on competitive analysis or literature reviews. Then they directly go for design or redesign of design solutions and then build a prototype and then evaluate the product. In the evaluation phase, the actual users might not give feedbacks for the prototypes rather either clients or others empathies and play role of users and give feedbacks. The bugs reduction is also involved in the evaluation stage and the final solutions are delivered. However, the clients or product owner might come up with the new requirement or user needs again after launching the product in the market.

This is an iterative process. Sometimes, this process exemplifies the user-centred design approach when designer empathizes the target audiences or clients and not evaluate the product based on user feedbacks.

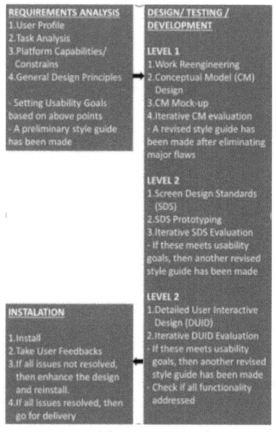

Fig. 3.2 Usability Engineering Lifecycle.

3. Usability Engineering Lifecycle

This follows the complete user-centred design process. There are five major steps involved in the usability engineering lifecycle (UEL) –

1) Requirements analysis
2) Design
3) Testing
4) Development
5) Installation

The UEL is very rigorous process in terms of user centric evaluation of mock-ups and prototypes. This is also an iterative process and it continues until the target users satisfied with the usability goals which was predefined at the initial stage of the UEL. The detail process is illustrated in the **Fig. 3.2**. This process is applicable for designing a software/ product. This process is an example of Agile UX process and it takes comparatively longer time than simple interaction design process.

4. Double Diamond Design Process

The double diamond (DD) design process was first proposed by Design Council, UK. Later, industry practitioners have applied this model for product, software and service experience design. The DD design process has four basic steps –

1) Discover (Requirement Analysis)
2) Define (Problem Statement)
3) Design and Development
4) Deliver

The Discover and Design phases are associated with the divergent thinking process; whereas, the define and deliver phases are related to convergent thinking process.

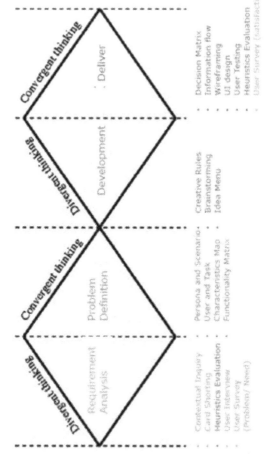

Fig. 3.3 Double Diamond UX process.

The divergent thinking enables identification of user needs or pains of target users as designers observing the situations with open mindset in the discovery phase. Designers are also welcoming various bold solutions at the design phase using divergent thought process. On the other side, define phase focuses on prioritization of problems or user needs through convergent thinking, because solutions for all the problems are not possible at the same time mainly due to constrains in time and resources. The convergent thinking process also reinforces the analysis of proposed solutions to find out the best and feasible solutions for the defined problem. For all these reasons this design process is widely accepted and applied in many industries.

If the UX design methods can be integrated with the DD design process, it will be better for understanding of upcoming UX designers. Please find the **Fig. 3.3** for DD with the UX design methods. Please remember there are few UX methods which can be applied in both the discover and delivery phases. For example, heuristics evaluation could be applied for problem identification for redesign the website as well as for ensuring usability of the website in delivery phase.

5. Goal Directed Design Process

The goal directed design process (GDDP) is pretty similar to usability lifecycle. It is an agile process used in mature product or IT firms for designing digital products. The major steps of this process include –

1) Research
2) Modeling
3) Requirements Definition
4) Design Framework
5) Design Refinement
6) Design Support

5.1. Research

The research involves following steps:

Scope: this step aims to define project goals and schedule with various concerns of objectives, timelines, financial constraints, process, milestones

Audit: this step aims to review existing work and products in the market. Various concerns like Business and marketing plans, branding strategy, market research, product portfolio plans, competitors, relevant technologies are covered.

Stakeholder Interviews: This step aims to understand product vision of the client, constraints, risks, opportunities, logistics, and end users.

User interviews & observations: this step helps to understand user needs and their behavior based on primary research findings. User types, their behaviors, attitudes, aptitudes, motivations, environments, tools, challenges etc. are key concerns in this step.

5.2. Modeling

In this phase, there are mainly two steps –

Making Personas: these are user and customer prototypes. The persona helps in understanding of patterns in user and customer behaviors, attitudes, aptitudes, goals, environments, tools, challenges etc.

Preparation of Other Models: these represent domain factors beyond individual users and customers. Workflows among multiple people, environments, artifacts etc. are major concerns in this step.

5.3. Requirements Definition

Context Scenarios: UX designers tell stories about ideal user experiences to highlight the product fit with the person's life and environment, and usefulness of the product to achieve their goals.

Requirements: defining requirements is actually describe the necessary capabilities of the product. Functional and data needs, user mental models, design imperatives, product vision, business requirements, technology etc. are the key concerns at this step.

5.4. Design Framework

Elements: Define manifestations of information and functionality Information such as functions, mechanisms, actions, domain object models.

Framework: Plan overall architecture of user experience. The UX designers can find out object relationships, they can do conceptual groupings, navigation sequencing, principles and patterns, flow, sketches, storyboards.

Key Path and Validation Scenarios: Elaborate how the user group interacts with the software or product. Define ways to fit interface design with an ideal sequence of user behaviors, and accommodate a diverse probable circumstance.

5.5. Design Refinement

Detailed design: In this stage designers generally refine their ideas and specify details of the interface design. Refinement and detailing of look and feel, phrases or terminologies, interface type and interactions, widgets, behavior, information architecture, data visualization, integration of brand value and identity, user experience, language, presentation of scenarios using storyboards are important activities in this stage.

5.6. Design Support

Design modification: Consider new limitations and timeframe. Sustaining conceptual integrity of the interface design under rapid change of technologies and its constraints.

Bibliography

1. Cooper, A., Reimann, R., & Cronin, D. (2007). *About face 3: the essentials of interaction design.* John Wiley & Sons.
2. Rogers, Y., Sharp, H., & Preece, J. (2011). *Interaction design: beyond human-computer interaction.* John Wiley & Sons.
3. Howard, T. J., Culley, S. J., & Dekoninck, E. (2008). Describing the creative design process by the integration of engineering design and cognitive psychology literature. *Design studies*, *29*(2), 160-180.
4. http://www.designcouncil.org.uk/webdav/harmonise?Page/@id=53&Session/@id=D_4jaHtwk0Hj7ve5elIToe&Document/@id=10149

***

CHAPTER 4

Essential Methods for UX Design

Key learnings -

- ❖ Methods for user requirement analysis for short-term and long-term UX projects
- ❖ Pros and cons of different UX methods
- ❖ Case examples on various UX methods

1. Literature Review

Literature review is a kind of secondary research. Literature review can be conducted using various search engines and digital libraries. Followings are commonly used for literature survey as authentic resources on HCI and UX design are available:

- Google Scholar
- Web of Science
- Science Direct (Elsevier)
- Scopus
- ACM Digital Library

- IEEE Xplore Digital Library
- Taylor and Francis Digital Library
- Springer Link Digital Library
- Etc.

There are many books, journals, periodicals etc. are available in these online resources. When UX designers have comparatively less time, they can utilize these online resources to understand the user behaviour, culture, socioeconomic status, system design concepts etc. and present all these data in a table like **Table 4.1**. User reviews from the Google play store or Apple app store can also represented as part of literature review like **Table 4.2**.

Disadvantage of this method include availability of direct user data or system concepts actually desired for the client project. However, the UX designer can get ideas about user behaviour, culture, socioeconomic status, and they can take inspiration regarding system design concepts for the desired solutions.

Table 4.1 Systematic Literate Survey.

Sources	Key Findings	Novel Function/ Process	Key take away
X et al. (1990)	A, B findings	Yes	F function can be utilized for client solution
Y and Z (2010)	A, C findings	No	F function is not novel / not fitting to the problem solution
Y (2020)	C, D findings	Yes	P process is useful for software / service design

Table 4.2 Systematic Sentiment analysis.

App Name	Functions	Comments	Ratings/ Usage	Sentiment/ Emotion
	A, B, C	I am very happy to use this app	*****	Positive
	A, X, Y	This app is useful but requires robust notification system	***	Moderate
	X, Y	I don't like the interface of this this app as its very basic and many important functions are missing in compare to other apps in this genre	*	Negative

2. User Sentiment Analysis based on Analytics and User Reviews

Now-a-days, user ratings and comments for different apps are available in various platforms such as Google play store, Apple App Store, e-commerce platforms (e.g. Amazon, Flipkart, Snapdeal etc.), Statista, Alexa Ranking, Google analytics etc. The UX designers can identify the functions of various apps along with user ratings and comments. Based on these parameters, they could identify user emotions and sentiments against a particular set of functions of the app.

This method is a part of competitor analysis and it is very useful when a UX designer need to provide quick solutions to clients. Following table might be useful for user sentiment analysis.

3. Task Analysis

Task analysis is very important method when designing a service design or any interface design. There are various aspects UX designers need to observe or highlight during task analysis –

- Task goals
- Steps and sub-steps (actions) involved in a task
- Information required to accomplish a task
- Any instructional support required for a task
- Stakeholder involved in a task
- Interactions of stakeholders with the tools used in a task
- Influence of the job environment where stakeholders are performing a task
- How coordination and interactions are happening while performing a task in a group
- Time required to accomplish a task
- Errors executed by stakeholder(s) while performing a task
- Effort (physical and mental) required for the task
- Risks involved in the task or any hazards causes by the task or task environment

The hierarchical task analysis and cognitive walkthrough are the commonly used methods for user task analysis. For hierarchical of task analysis, UX designers can break the entire task goal into sub-task or sub-sub-task levels and further they can analyses the problems are instructional requirements at various levels of task. A proforma for hierarchical task analysis is presented in **Fig. 4.1**.

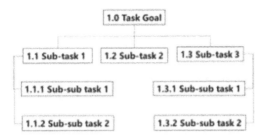

Fig. 4.1 Proforma for hierarchical task analysis.

This technique sometimes also helps to prepare information architecture. A case study on hierarchical task analysis is presented in the **Fig. 4.2**.

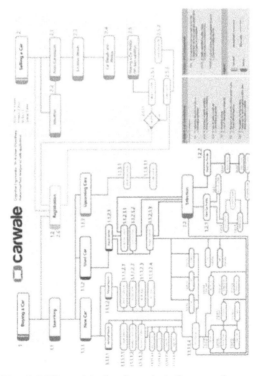

Fig. 4.2 Hierarchical task analysis for carwale.com

4. User Interview

The interview is a qualitative user research method and it could be conducted in various setups –

- One-to-one at studio
- One-to-one at field
- Telephonic
- Online (audio/ video call)

Interviewer need to use audio recorder, video camera, notebooks, questionnaire etc. to record the interview data. An UX researcher should at least take 15 interviews from the target audiences to get most of the insights.

At the time of user interview, UX designers records the demographic and socio-cultural details at the initial stage, and then go for asking questions related to different use cases and scenarios related to initial problem statements either defined by clients or a designer. User interview gives many interesting and unique insights related to user problems and needs. Based on the responses get in user interview, UX designers might also gathers options for multiple choice questions which are generally utilized in questionnaire survey to quantify the user responses.

Generally, use researchers ask open ended questions to the target users or stakeholders. It is challenging to analyze the user responses get through open-ended questions. Further, quantification and generalization of finding is difficult based user interview.

5. Affinity Analysis

Affinity analysis is the technique for analysis of data collected from either user interview or diary method.

Fig. 4.3 The UX researchers are preparing affinity map using chart paper and sticky notes of different colour.

Affinity analysis is based on 'Grounded Theory' in which user researchers are trying to build a theory based on pattern analysis and inductive reasoning. Affinity charts are useful tool for the same. When user researchers ask open ended questions to users, users might answer a particular question either in differently or the same answers using different words. Affinity analysis then helps UX researches to segregate users' responses into different clusters and then in establishment of relations among different responses in a meaningful manner to a particular context of the user study. Please see **Fig. 4.3** for affinity map. This method gives insights in a systematic way and useful for understanding of user behaviour. However, it is not possible to generalize findings for larger group of audience until user researchers going for hypothesis testing after this analysis. Now-a-days UX researchers are collaborating online and conducting affinity analysis online using Lucid chart, Miro etc.

6. Card Shorting & Information Architecture

Meaningful headings and easy terminology are important for understanding of menu of many software or apps. In addition, hierarchy of information should be expressive as per the information demand of the target users. Therefore, it is important to design menu and address the information architecture of websites or other application from user point of view. The car shorting technique enables understanding of users understanding of different keywords used to design menu of an application and also hierarchy of information and its flow, useful for Information Architecture (IA) of a software or websites.

There are two types of card shorting techniques –

1)   Open Card Shorting
2)   Close Card Shorting

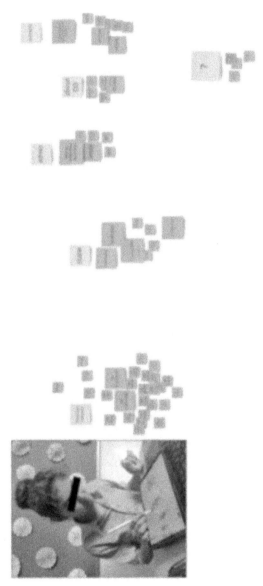

Fig. 4.4 Card Shorting by the user using Miro.

Fig. 4.5 Information Architecture based on close card shorting method.

In case of open card shorting technique, users have complete freedom to choose any keywords that they think suitable for a particular software menu; after that users can arrange different items of the menu as per the information demand. On the other side, designers decide the name of different items of the menu and then they ask target users to arrange these items as per the information demand to pursue a task (Please see **Fig. 4.4**).

Both these techniques are very useful to prepare information architecture based on the frequency of similar arrangement of different icons of the menu by a group of target users (Please see the example as in **Fig. 4.5**). Based on the user feedback, sometimes designers are also deciding the terminology of menu items.

Table 4.3 Results of heuristics evaluation.

#1: Visibility of system status
When we click back button it directly takes you to
the 1st page leads to misuderstanding and extra work
 #2: Match between system and the real world
common laungauge is english only
#3: User control and freedom
User doesnot have freedom to cancel the request once made
#4: Consistency and standards
thetre are more than 6 ways to search leads to discripency
#5: Error prevention
There is no return button
#6: Recognition rather than recall
there are a lot options are provided which leads to confusion
#7: Flexibility and efficiency of use
3 offers option 5 match option 6 search option
and there are 3 layers of apply to apply anything
#8: Aesthetic and minimalist design
first 3 screens are minimalist
#9: Help users recognize, diagnose, and recover from errors
Autofill is not there and app doesnot support different language
#10: Help and documentation
help icon leads you to other screen, last screen doesnt remember your inputs

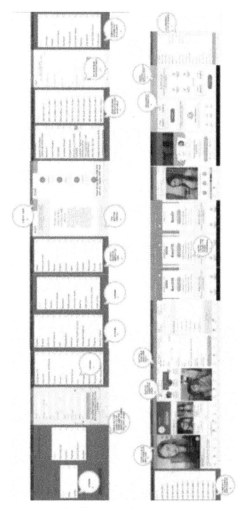

Fig. 4.6 Screens of shadi.com mobile app that have problems in terms of various heuristics.

7. Heuristics Evaluation

Heuristics evaluation is an expert evaluation method in which UX designers or human factors experts are seating together to evaluate the UI of different products or software.

In this method, a set of usability heuristics or human factors principles are considered to achieve to usability goals. UX designers are utilizing this method for the both requirements analysis during redesign exercise and to evaluate the newly designed interfaces. Nielsen's 10 heuristics principles are very famous and widely used by UX designers. Although there are other heuristics proposed by other researchers like Bastien and Scapin (1995), Yong et al. 2006.

Results of heuristics evaluation of shadi.com mobile app is presented in **Table 4.3** and interface related problems are also highlighted in **Fig. 4.6**.

8. User Survey

User survey is a user data collection method generally utilized for either user need and pain points analysis or post launch product/software/service experience survey. A user survey is typically conducted using a standard questionnaire. User researchers takes inputs from user interview during standardization of questionnaire. A questionnaire includes consent of the user, demographic information and mostly either multiple choice questions or scale-based questions (e.g. Likert scale) to record the user responses about the design deliverables. Many UX researchers are now user Google forms, survey monkey etc. to conduct the user surveys.

9. Contextual Inquiry

Contextual inquiry is a mixed method. The contextual study is also an equivalent method for user ethnography. It has two parts – 1) Observational study and Contextual Interviews.

During observational study, the UX researchers need to visit the site where user is performing their job. The critical observations on physical environment, workings tools or gadgets, task flow, information exchange, and culture. After the critical observation, user researchers generally conduct interviews with users at the work environment and ask questions related to user task /job. This phase is known as contextual interviews.

At the end of this process, UX designers go for depicting five pictorial models to understand the problems related to the user task. These models are –

1. *Flow model:* It is related to information flow and exchange during the task
2. *Sequence model:* It is related to the task sequence
3. *Cultural model:* It is related to the socio-economic or job culture
4. *Physical model:* It is related to the physical environment where the task is performed by users
5. *Artifact model:* It is related to the tools or devices are used during the task by users

10. Focus Group

In the focus group study, the demographically diverse group of users' reactions are studied either in a guided manner or open discussions about a new product or software or services to determine the reactions that can be expected from a larger population of target users. It is a kind of qualitative user research in which group interviews are conducted to know about the perceptions, opinions, beliefs, and attitudes towards a product, service, concept, advertisement, idea, or packaging; from the target users.

In a guided focus group study, a moderator helps to guide users to focus on the use cases and design solutions. During focus group discussions, video cameras and microphones are also used to record responses of the representative user group.

11. Think Aloud Protocol

This is a kind of verbal protocol analysis for testing of product or software interfaces and this is a task-based interface evaluation method. In a traditional think aloud protocol, users are asked to articulate their views or problem encountered during the performance of the task. However, this protocol has some flaw such as the actual task completion time never be calculated as the users start talking about the problems of the interface in between the performance of the task. Therefore, most of the UX designers are now using retrospective think aloud protocol in which users are articulating about their experiences immediately after completion of the task. Although, there is another loop-hole is aroused with retrospective think aloud protocol i.e. users often forget about problems that they faced during performance of the task if it takes longer time to accomplish. Therefore, it is always better to split the long task into small fragments and then users should be recruited for retrospective think aloud study.

12. Usability Testing

Usability testing is important to ensure the usability aspects of the software or product interfaces. Usability testing required experimental design either with same group of users (within subject study) or with different group of users (between subject study), for two or more interface designs. It is possible to compare usability of an existing design with the modified design (A-B testing) or to compare usability of various interface design iterations with built prototypes. There are various standard usability testing questionnaires that are available such as System Usability Scale (SUS) (Please see **Table 4.4**), Perceived Usefulness (PU) Scale and Perceived Ease of Use (PEoU) scale (Please see **Table 4.5**) etc.

Table 4.4 System Usability Scale.

SL No.	Items
1	I think that I would like to use this system frequently.
2	I found the system unnecessarily complex.
3	I thought the system was easy to use.
4	I think that I would need the support of a technical person to be able to use this system.
5	I found the various functions in this system were well integrated.
6	I thought there was too much inconsistency in this system.
7	I would imagine that most people would learn to use this system very quickly.
8	I found the system very cumbersome to use.
9	I felt very confident using the system.
10	I needed to learn a lot of things before I could get going with this system.

Usability experts generally take ratings on either 5 points or 7 points likers scales, e.g.'1' means strongly disagree, '3' means neutral and '5' means strongly agree to above sentences in case of 5 points Likert scale.

Table 4.5 Perceived Usefulness and Perceived Ease of Use Scales.

SL No.	Items of Perceived Usefulness
1	This interface/ product helps me to do the job more effective way
2	This interface/ product helps me be more productive in achieving the task goal
3	This interface/ product is useful
4	This interface gives me more control over the software / product
5	It makes my task easier utilizing this interface/ product
6	It meets my needs for my job

SL No.	Items of Perceived Ease of Use
1	This interface/ product is easy to use
2	This interface/ product is user friendly
3	It requires the fewest step to accomplish my task
4	It is flexible to use
5	Use of this interface/ product is effortless
6	I can use this bottle without any written instruction

Usability experts generally take ratings on either 5 points or 7 points Likert scales, e.g.'1' means strongly disagree, '3' means neutral and '5' means strongly agree to above sentences in case of 5 points Likert scale.

13. NASA-TLX Scale

This scale is generally used for measurement of cognitive workload. Full form of NASA-TLX is NASA Task Load Index. This scale was developed by Ames Research Centre, NASA. Actually, the cognitive workload is faced by user due to six major factors such as –

1) *Mental Demand* – It is related to the needs of perceptual processing (e.g. thinking, calculation, remembering, searching etc.)

2) *Physical Demand* – It is related to the physical activities (e.g. clicking, scrolling, pushing, pulling, swiping etc.)

3) *Temporal Demand* – It is related to the time pressure users feels or rate or pace of work / task.

4) *Performance* – It is related to the successful accomplishment of the task goals and its associated level of satisfaction.

5) *Effort* – It is associated with the both mental and physical hardness to accomplish the task performance.

6) *Frustration Level* – It is related to the insecurity, stress, irritation etc. faced while performing the task.

It is possible to measure cognitive workload if we can measure the level of these six factors using a 20 points scale for a particular task might be utilizing a product or software. However, all these factors are not equally important for all kind of tasks. It might be context specific. For example, arithmetic calculation task required more mental demand that the physical demand; whereas gardening require more physical demand than the mental demand. Therefore, priority ratings are important while measuring cognitive workload and need to ask which factor is more relevant for a particular task, could be ensure by asking users about the factors in 15 different combinations (Please see **Table 4.6**), as there are 6 factors related to cognitive workload in this scale. The NASA-TLX score could be calculated using the **Table 4.7**.

Table 4.6 Combinations with different factors for priority ratings in NASA-TLX scale.

SL. No.	Combinations
1	Mental Demand Vs. Physical Demand
2	Mental Demand Vs. Temporal Demand
3	Mental Demand Vs. Performance
4	Mental Demand Vs. Effort
5	Mental Demand Vs. Frustration Level
6	Physical Demand Vs. Temporal Demand
7	Physical Demand Vs. Performance
8	Physical Demand Vs. Effort
9	Physical Demand Vs. Frustration Level
10	Temporal Demand Vs. Performance
11	Temporal Demand Vs. Effort

12	Temporal Demand Vs. Frustration Level
13	Performance Vs. Effort
14	Performance Vs. Frustration Level
15	Effort Vs. Frustration Level

Table 4.7 An example for calculation of NASA-TLX score.

Factors	Raw Score (RS) (Max: 20 pts)	Tally Marking (TM) (Max: 5)	Weighted Scores (WS) (RS ×TM)
Mental Demand	e.g. 18	e.g. 卌 (5)	90
Physical Demand	e.g. 15	e.g. ||| (3)	45
Temporal Demand	e.g. 15	e.g.	(1)	15
Performance	e.g. 15	e.g. || (2)	30
Effort	e.g. 15	e.g. |||| (4)	60
Frustration Level	e.g. 8	0	0
NASA-TLX Score = ((Σ WS) / 15) = (240/15) = 16			

14. SAM Scale

The self-assessment manikin (SAM) is widely accepted scale for measurement of affective or emotional state of users. It has three items with 5 points scales viz. happiness scale (happy vs. unhappy), excitement scale (excited vs. calm) and bodily control scale (controlled vs. in control) (Please see **Fig. 4.7**). It is possible to measure mood or any affective responses against design solutions based on subjective user ratings. During statistical analysis, UX designers need to reverse the code of happiness and excitement scales when they are expecting the positive affect for a design deliverable (s).

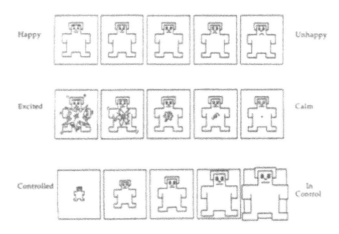

Fig. 4.7 The self-assessment manikin (SAM) scale.

15. Basic User Data Analytics using Excel

It is possible to analyse the user data using Microsoft Excel. Basic statistics such as average ratings (on SAM/Likert scale) for user responses on different parameters, calculation of frequencies of user responses, percentages of particular user response category etc. can be calculated after feeding the data in an excel sheet. Designers need to explore Formulas tab in MS excel. Designers can also plot the various chart chart using Insert tab. For instance, bar chart on user responses about bikes are presented in **Fig. 4.8.**

Fig. 4.8 Bar chart on quality of bikes.

16. User Data Visualization Methods [Persona/ Story Board (Scenario)/ Consumer Journey Map/ Empathy Map/ Other Infographics]

The UX designers can go for various illustration techniques to tell the user stories. It is very crucial to understand user characteristics before going to design the interface. The representation of persona is helping to understand user profile. Typically, the persona is a prototypic representation of a target user group, and designer can make persona using online tools like https://www.hubspot.com/make-my-persona. User storyboard and user journey map are very useful for portraying user problems, requirements, different scenarios or use cases and stories (**Fig. 4.9**). The consumer journey map displays step-by-step procedure for particular task or process along with various touch points and user experiences or emotions (**Fig. 4.10**).

Fig. 4.9 User storyboard on bike purchase.

Fig. 4.10 Consumer Journey Map on Bike purchase process.

Fig. 4.11 Empathy map of user group targeted for bike selling.

The empathy mapping (Please see **Fig. 4.11**) is a visual representation technique of data collected from interview or user survey with open ended questions.In an empathy map UX researchers generally highlight the feelings of users, perception of users and their perspectives regarding the task utilizing a software or product or tools.

Bibliography

1. Hendrickson, A. R., Massey, P. D., & Cronan, T. P. (1993). On the test-retest reliability of perceived usefulness and perceived ease of use scales. *MIS quarterly*, 227-230.
2. Bangor, A., Kortum, P. T., & Miller, J. T. (2008). An empirical evaluation of the system usability scale. *Intl. Journal of Human–Computer Interaction*, *24*(6), 574-594.
3. Hart, S. G. (2006, October). NASA-task load index (NASA-TLX); 20 years later. In *Proceedings of the human factors and ergonomics society annual meeting* (Vol. 50, No. 9, pp. 904-908). Sage CA: Los Angeles, CA: Sage publications.
4. https://www.alliedacademies.org/articles/emotion-analysis-using-sam-selfassessment-manikin-scale.html#:~:text=The%20Self%2DAssessment%20Manikin%20(SAM)%20is%20a%20pictographic%20scale,on%20perceived%20emotion%20%5B9%5D.
5. Rosenbaum, M. S., Otalora, M. L., & Ramírez, G. C. (2017). How to create a realistic customer journey map. *Business Horizons*, *60*(1), 143-150.
6. Ferreira, B., Silva, W., Oliveira, E., & Conte, T. (2015, July). Designing Personas with Empathy Map. In *SEKE* (Vol. 152).
7. Bynion, T. M., & Feldner, M. T. (2017). Self-assessment manikin. *Encyclopedia of personality and individual differences*, 1-3.

***

CHAPTER 5

Visual Design Strategy

Key learnings -

- ❖ Way of Navigation Design
- ❖ Graphic User Interface Design
- ❖ Semiotic approaches to UI design

1. Wireframing and Navigation Design

Wireframes are basic layouts for UI design of websites or apps (See **Fig. 5.1**). Remember, the IA or understanding of task flow (or activity diagram) is important before wireframing. Wireframes helps UX designers to understand the navigation and interaction of the interface along with visual hierarchy and ways of content presentation. The UI designers generally don't put actual contents during wireframe design, rather they put dummy images or texts (e.g. Laureum Ipsums). Wireframes give idea how UI will look. Many UI designers first go for hand drawn wireframe and then they go for illustration so wireframes.

Generally, UX designers plan for different navigation types to navigate from one page to other pages. Navigation using menu and buttons are most common. There are different kinds of navigations exist for webs, these are –

- Primary menu bar
- Secondary (inverted L type) menu bar
- Footer menu
- Hamburger menu
- Drawer type menu
- Buttons
- Hyperlink text
- Vertical Scrolling
- Horizontal Scrolling
- Wizards
- Sitemap etc.

The mobile navigations involve –

- Hamburger menu
- Footer Menu Bar
- Buttons
- Swipe
- Scrolling
- List
- Tiles
- Hyperlink text
- Etc.

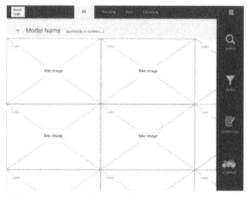

Fig. 5.1 Illustrated Wireframes for a customized bike purchase app.

2. Prototyping

Prototypes are functional model of UI. There are three kinds of prototypes –

- Low fidelity
- Medium fidelity
- High fidelity

Paper prototypes are low fidelity prototypes in which functionalities of a mobile app or websites are showcased through visuals. Wireframe layouts are generally considered as low fidelity prototype (Please see **Fig. 5.1**). In case of medium fidelity prototype, prototypes generally have interactive controls or buttons, however these are not fully functional. The UX designer can use Adobe XD, Figma, Sketch, Invision, Marvel App, Balsamiq, Justinmind etc. to design interactive medium fidelity prototype. However, for UI screen design, visual designers often use the Adobe Photoshop and Adobe Illustrator. The medium fidelity prototype doesn't connect to the database or a server to fetch the data and represent it on the UI. High fidelity prototyping requires software development kits or programming skills and this kind of prototypes are fully functional and it is connected with database (saved in either local server or cloud server).

3. Visual Design Guidelines

Different IT giants like Google, Microsoft, Apple, IBM etc. have their own design guidelines for UI design these are –

- Google Material Design Guidelines for Android apps design
- IOS Guidelines for Apple Store apps design
- Windows Guidelines for Windows app design

All these guidelines consider different aspects of design such as –

- Scree sizes
- Icon sizes
- Resolutions
- Margins and Layouts
- Responsiveness (e.g. same app for different device platforms such as mobile, tablet etc.)
- Font types
- Font sizes
- Guidelines for differently abled persons

In India, UI design is comparatively flexible. Designers of many startups and consultancy companies do UI design as per their own convenience. However, it is always good to set own guidelines to maintain the consistency and standards of design solutions.

4. Visual Design Explorations

The UI designers always need to go for visual design explorations (See **Fig. 5.2** and **Fig. 5.3**) as much as it possible based on timeline of the project. They can explore the following elements and try for various compositions –

- Colour Pallets
- Typefaces
- Iconography
- Photographs

The colour pallet selection often depends on –

- Brand Identity (logo/ trademark etc._
- Product / Service Theme (e.g. summer collection/ suit, winter collection/ suit etc.)
- Mood board selected by client (e.g. predefined emotions and keywords represented through a collage of similar images)
- Inspiration board suggested by client (e.g. motivated by colour of key competitors)

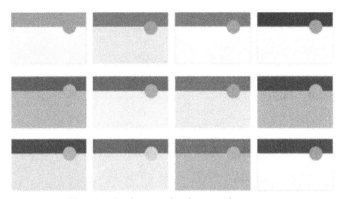

Fig. 5.2 Background colour explorations.

There are different kinds of typefaces (sheriff and sans) designers are using for UI design. However, following points we need to consider –

- Legibility (visual clarity of a single alphabet) of the selected typeface(s)
- Readability (visual clarity of alphabets in words or paragraph in text) of the selected typeface(s)
- Font colour in respect to background colour
- Font sizes for different screen sizes for different devices, especially in case of responsive devices.

Roboto, Segoe UI, Myriad Pro, Verdana, Helvetica, Leelawadee UI, Lucida Sans, Yu Gothic etc. are commonly used fonts for UI design.

Icons are very useful elements to in the UI (see **Fig. 5.3**). Many UI designers adopt icons from different repositories (e.g. Google material design icons). Visual designers also design icons sometime applying visual design principles (e.g. gestalt laws). They need to ensure the following things before icon selection for interfaces –

- Familiarity of icons
- Understandability of icons
- Legibility of icons in respect to their size
- Readability of text embedded in the icon
- Icon colour

Fig. 5.3 Exploration of colour of icons.

Now-a-days many software applications are very rich of photographs. In this context, use of photographs should be meaningful to the use context. The UX designers either go for a metaphoric (indirect) representation or analogic (partially direct) representation or direct representation of context of product or software through photographs.

5. Semiotic Approaches to UI design

Based on the knowledge in the different domains of semantics and cognitive human factors UI designers now following different ontologies (a set of concepts and categories in a subject area) for website design. These ontologies are –

1. *Institution Ontology* is the knowledge concerning the institution or an organization staying behind the website (See **Fig. 5.4**)

Fig. 5.4 Banner of the web interface shows Institutional ontology.

Fig. 5.5 Facebook interface area which is highlighted with rectangle shows the topic ontology.

2. *Topic Ontology* is the knowledge concerning the particular topic or subject the organization or an institution generally talks about (See **Fig. 5.5**).

3. *Context Ontology* is the knowledge not directly related to the topics the website talks about but

relevant for making the dialogue possible and comprehensible (See **Fig. 5.6**).

Fig. 5.6 Context ontology of Facebook is highlighted with rectangles.

4. *Website Ontology* is the knowledge regarding the website in itself (See **Fig. 5.7**).

Fig. 5.7 Website ontology of Facebook webapp is highlighted with rectangles.

5. *Internet Ontology* is the knowledge of concepts, skills, conventions shared among typical web surfers or among people familiar with web browsing in general (See **Fig. 5.8**).

6. *Web Domain Ontology* is the knowledge shared among websites belonging to the same sector/ domain or "business sector" (See **Fig. 5.9**).

Fig. 5.8 Internet ontology of Facebook is highlighted with rectangles.

Fig. 5.9 Web Domain Ontology of Facebook is highlighted with rectangles.

7. *Common Sense Ontology* is the set of concepts belonging to the common background, and semiotic

units can count on this shared knowledge to trigger understanding (See **Fig. 5.10**).

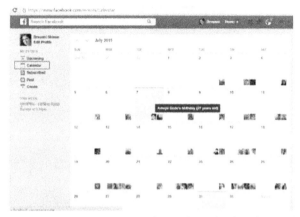

Fig. 5.10 Common Sense Ontology of Facebook is highlighted with rectangle.

Bibliography

1. Kalbach, J. (2007). *Designing Web navigation: Optimizing the user experience.* "O'Reilly Media, Inc.".
2. Codognet, P. (2005). The semiotics of the web. *Leonardo, 35*(1), 1-18.
3. Chandler, D. (1994). *Semiotics for beginners.*
4. Rogers, Y., Sharp, H., & Preece, J. (2011). *Interaction design: beyond human-computer interaction.* John Wiley & Sons.
5. Benyon, D. (2014). Designing interactive systems: A comprehensive guide to HCI, UX and interaction design.

***

CHAPTER 6

Elementary ideas on AR, VR and XR based interfaces

Key learnings -

- ❖ Differences between augmented reality (AR), virtual reality (VR) and extended reality (XR)
- ❖ Scopes of application of AR, VR, and XR for UX design in various contexts
- ❖ Heuristics for AR and VR based interfaces

1. Definition of AR and Case Examples

Augmented reality systems are having real environment and artificial objects are portrayed on the interface. For instance, is a customer want to purchase a furniture online, an AR enabled e-commerce app (Please see Fig. 6.1) might help to understand the customer to analyse the suitability of the furniture in respect to room colour, size, carpet area etc. In another example, an AR app might help to scan small animal bodies (e.g. mice) to identify tiny vital organs like thymus gland as many medical researchers are struggling to identify this small tiny gland. The AR interfaces have various applications such as e-learning (AR enabled books for kids and higher studies), instruction design and training, application for colour blinds etc.

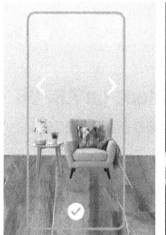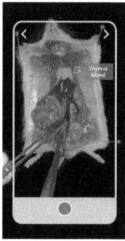

Fig. 6.1 The AR apps (Left: online shopping, Right: Tiny organ detection for mice).

2. Heuristics for AR interface evaluations

The heuristics evaluation of any AR is possible using a set of heuristics have been proposed by Ko, Chang & Ji (2013). According to them, key heuristics are –

User-information: "The user-information group consists of principles related to providing information to users such as visual information, classified menu structure, and familiarity with expression".

User-cognitive: "The user-cognitive group consists of principles related to cognitive aspects required for users to minimize memory loads, react as expected, and learn applications easily".

User-support: "The user-support group consists of principles related to user support: providing useful information, reducing errors, handling, and personalizing".

Heuristics	Problem (Y/N)	Recommendation
User-information		
Multimodality		
Enjoyment		
Familiarity		
Visibility		
Hierarchy		
Defaults		
User-cognitive		
Recognition		
Predictability		
Learnability		
Consistency		
User-interaction		
Error Management		
Help and documentation		
User control		
Personalization		
User-support		
Feedback		
Direct manipulation		
Responsiveness		
Low physical effort		
User-usage		
Context based		
Exiting		
Navigation		
Availability		

Table 6.1 Parameters for heuristics evaluation of AR apps.

User-interaction: "The user-interaction group consists of principles related to interaction between users and applications, such as providing feedback with minimum manipulation".

User-usage: "The user-usage group consists of principles related to actual usage, which include reactions appropriate for surrounding situations and methods to use or stop the applications easily".

A table for heuristics evaluation of AR app is presented as follows (**Table 6.1**):

3. Definitions of VR & XR, and Case Examples

The virtual reality (VR) means a simulated environment with or without 3D virtual objects. For example, artificial rain fall in a room is an example of simulation of virtual environment in a physical space. In addition, virtual environment might entirely be CAD (computer aided design) generated. In case of many mobile VR apps like In Mind VR both the objects and environment are CAD generated. Another example of a mobile VR platform is the mobile VR app for national heritage sites for promotion of tourism in the country, presented in **Fig. 6.2.**

Fig. 6.2 The mobile VR app for immersive experiences of national heritage sites.

The extended reality (XR) is a multimodal reality platform in which humans are able to interact with the virtual objects through joysticks, phantom omni like tactile feedback generating robots, based on hand gesture recognition system, voice recognition systems or any other sensor-based biofeedback systems. In case of XR, user interface is more natural. This kind of user interface is also known as the natural user interface.

4. Heuristics for VR or XR interface evaluations

According to Sutcliffe and Gault (2004), following heuristics are important for VR interface evaluation.

- *Natural engagement*: "Interaction should approach the user's expectation of interaction in the real world as far as possible. Ideally, the user should be unaware that the reality is virtual. Interpreting this heuristic will depend on the naturalness requirement and the user's sense of presence and engagement".

- *Compatibility with the user's task and domain*: "The virtual environment (VE) and behaviour of objects should correspond as closely as possible to the user's expectation of real-world objects; their behaviour; and affordances for task action".

- *Natural expression of action*: "The representation of the self/presence in the VE should allow the user to act and explore in a natural manner and not restrict normal physical actions. This design quality may be limited by the available devices. If haptic feedback is absent, natural expression inevitably suffers".

- *Close coordination of action and representation*: "The representation of the self/ presence and behaviour manifest in the VE should be faithful to the user's actions. Response time between user movement and update of the VE display should be less than 200 ms to avoid motion sickness problems".

- *Realistic feedback*: "The effect of the user's actions on virtual world objects should be immediately visible and conform to the laws of physics and the user's perceptual expectations".

- *Faithful viewpoints*: "The visual representation of the virtual world should map to the user's normal perception, and the viewpoint change by head movement should be rendered without delay".

- *Navigation and orientation support*: "The users should always be able to find where they are in the VE and return to known, preset positions. Unnatural actions such as fly-through surfaces may help but these have to be judged in a trade-off with naturalness (see heuristics 1 and 2)".

- *Clear entry and exit points*: "The means of entering and exiting from a virtual world should be clearly communicated".

- *Consistent departures*: "When design compromises are used, they should be consistent and clearly marked, e.g. cross-modal substitution and power actions for navigation".

- *Support for learning*: "Active objects should be cued and if necessary, explain themselves to promote learning of Ves".

- *Clear turn-taking*: "Where system initiative is used it should be clearly signaled and conventions established for turn-taking".

- *Sense of presence*: "The user's perception of engagement and being in a 'real' world should be as natural as possible".

Table 6.2 helps for heuristics evaluation of the VR/XR interfaces.

Table 6.2 Heuristics for VR interface assessment.

Sl. No.	Heuristics	Problems (Y/N)	Recommendation
1	Natural engagement		
2	Compatibility with the user's task and domain		
3	Natural expression of action		
4	Close coordination of action and representation		
5	Realistic feedback		
6	Faithful viewpoints		
7	Navigation and orientation support		
8	Clear entry and exit points		
9	Consistent departures		
10	Support for learning		
11	Clear turn-taking		
12	Sense of presence		

5. Preproduction, Production and Prototyping

Any AR or VR projects involve three major steps –

Preproduction – It is related to the planning of interface including understanding of requirements, concept sketches, storyboards, wireframing, interaction type selection etc.

Production – It involves generation of 3D assets or gathering ready assets for environments, objects, 3D shooting, Screen design, lighting design, sound design etc.

Prototyping – It involved integration of all assets on a game engine (e.g. Unity) or SDK (e.g. Google android SDK)

All these steps aiming to impressiveness (sometimes called presence) which is defined as a psychological state characterized by perceiving oneself to be enveloped by, included in, and interacting with an artificial environment that provides a continuous stream of stimuli and experiences.

Bibliography

1. Aukstakalnis, S. (2016). *Practical augmented reality: A guide to the technologies, applications, and human factors for AR and VR.* Addison-Wesley Professional.

2. Ohlenburg, J., Herbst, I., Lindt, I., Fröhlich, T., & Broll, W. (2004, November). The MORGAN framework: enabling dynamic multi-user AR and VR projects. In *Proceedings of the ACM symposium on Virtual reality software and technology* (pp. 166-169).

3. Speicher, M., Hall, B. D., & Nebeling, M. (2019, May). What is mixed reality?. In *Proceedings of the 2019 CHI Conference on Human Factors in Computing Systems* (pp. 1-15).

4. Billinghurst, M., & Kato, H. (1999, March). Collaborative mixed reality. In *Proceedings of the First International Symposium on Mixed Reality* (pp. 261-284).

5. Milgram, P., & Kishino, F. (1994). A taxonomy of mixed reality visual displays. *IEICE TRANSACTIONS on Information and Systems*, *77*(12), 1321-1329.

6. Goebel, M., Hirose, M., & Rosenblum, L. (2001). Today's VR. *IEEE Computer Graphics and Applications*, *21*(6), 22-24.

7. Ko, S. M., Chang, W. S., & Ji, Y. G. (2013). Usability principles for augmented reality applications in a

smartphone environment. *International Journal of Human-Computer Interaction*, *29*(8), 501-515.

8. Sutcliffe, A., & Gault, B. (2004). Heuristic evaluation of virtual reality applications. *Interacting with computers*, *16*(4), 831-849.

***

CHAPTER 7

Tangible User Interfaces

Key learnings -

❖ Fundamentals of tangible user interface (TUI) design

❖ Scopes of application of tangible interface design framework in various context

❖ Sensors and microprocessors

1. Definition of TUI

The tangible interface means any kind of physical interface and thus tangible user interface (TUI) is based on interaction with the elements of physical interface. The journey of tangible user interface design has been started with industrial display and control design for different machines. Previously, tangible interaction refers to interaction with physical controls such as switches, MCV, Jumpers, handles, gear levers, etc. along with some displays like analog meters, LED lights or bulbs etc. With advancements of electronics and embedded systems, it is now possible to control the systems using different sensors and microcontrollers. In modern time, 'Tangible Interface' also denotes systems that rely on

- physicality
- embodied interaction
- tangible representation of data
- embeddedness in real space, and augmentation of physical spaces.

The strategy for design and development of this kind of sensor-based interface has been discussed in this chapter.

2. Framework for TID

The famous tangible interface design framework (See **Fig. 7.1**) which was proposed by Eva Hornecker (2006). According to her, tangible interactions are possible through –

- Tangible manipulation
- Spatial Interaction
- Embodied Facilitation
- Expressive Representation

The tangible manipulation is possible to achieve through –

o *Haptic direct manipulation* which means touching, feeling and moving important elements of the interface
o *Lightweight Interaction* means rapid feedback during interaction or small experimental moves exerted by users.
o *Isomorph Effects* mean understanding of the relation between actions and their effects

Spatial interaction means tangible interaction is embedded in real space and interaction therefore occurring by movement in space. The spatial interaction is possible through –

o *Inhabited Space*: Meeting between users and objects in a meaningful space
o *Configurable Materials*: Ability of users to configure the space at all and appropriate it by doing so
o *Non-fragmented Visibility*: Every user should able to see changes that are happening in the surroundings and follow the visual references
o *Full-Body Interaction*: User should able to use their whole body
o *Performative Action:* User should able to communicate something through their body movement while doing what they supposed to do.

Tangible Manipulation	Spatial Interaction	Embodied Facilitation	Expressive Representation
Haptic Direct Manipulation	Inhabited Space	Embodied Constraints	Representational Significance
	Configurable Materials		
Lightweight Interaction	Non-fragmented Visibility	Multiple Access Points	Externalization
	Full Body Interaction		
Isomorph Effects	Performative Action	Tailored Representations	Perceived Coupling

Fig. 7.1 Framework for tangible interface design.

The embodied facilitation highlights the arrangement of physical objects and space affects and directs emerging user group behavior. This is possible through –

o *Embodied Constraints:* The physical set-up should lead users to collaborate by subtly constraining their behavior.

o *Multiple Access Points*: The all users able to understand the changes in surrounding environment and get their hands on the central objects of interest

o *Tailored Representation:* The representation should build on users' experience and it should connect with their experience and skills and invite them into interaction

The material and digital representations employed by tangible interaction systems, their expressiveness and legibility are focused under expressive representation. This is possible through –

o *Representational significance*: The representation of the interface should be meaningful and have long-lasting importance and the physical and digital representations of the same strength and salience.

o *Externalization*: Users should able to think and talk with or through objects, using them as props to act with. They should able to give discussions a focus and provide a record of decisions.

o *Perceived Coupling*: There should be a clear link between what users do and what happens. In addition, the physical and digital representations seemingly naturally coupled.

3. Arduino and different Sensors for TID

In tangible and embodied interfaces, designers are applying different sensors such as IR sensors, ultrasonic sensors, RFIDs, temperature sensor, Ph sensor, humidity sensor, piezoelectric sensor, vibration sensor etc. the IR sensors are generally applied as a proximity (distance) sensor or tracking lines for guided movement. The ultrasonic sensors can be measures distance or proximity. RFIDs are useful for identifying objects or tagging objects. Temperature sensor can be used for environmental monitoring, soil temperature measurement etc. The Ph sensor can be measured for soil quality check, food quality check, water quality check etc. Humidity sensor is useful for environmental monitoring, soil moisture check etc. The piezoelectric sensor can be useful for measurement of weight or pressure. The vibration sensor can be used for generating tactile messages or feedbacks. All these sensors can be integrated with Arduino which is a microcontroller having ATmega 328 microprocessor. This microprocessor can take inputs from different sensors and process the input signals to generate a fruitful output. There are various kind of Arduino present in the market and people are using them for different purposes (See **Fig. 7.2**). We can also fit a display unit (e.g. LCD display, or LED) with Arduino to observe the output. A designer can easily write computing programs in the Arduino open source software (Sketch) in embedded C language.

4.   Case Study: Blinking LED

A simple experiment can be conducted by designers to glow and blink LED lights using Arduino. One can try to run following programme using sketch software to do the same after having a setup with Arduino.

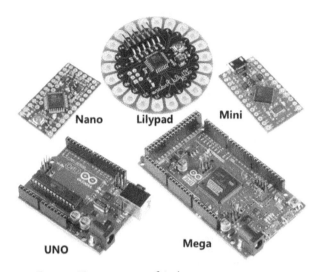

Fig. 7.2 Various types of Arduino microprocessor.

4.1. Programme for blinking lights in Arduino

```
*/

    // the setup function runs once when you press reset or
    power the board

    void setup() {

    // initialize digital pin LED_BUILTIN as an output.
    pinMode (LED_BUILTIN, OUTPUT);
}

// the loop function runs over and over again forever
void loop () {
    digitalWrite(LED_BUILTIN, HIGH); // turn the LED
on (HIGH is the voltage level)
    delay (1000); // wait for a second
```

digitalWrite (LED_BUILTIN, LOW); // turn the LED off by making the voltage LOW

delay (1000); // wait for a second

}

Beginners can know mor about different sensors and try different Arduino based tangible interface projects from the following YouTube link: https://www.youtube.com/watch?v=NePXqRwvmbs

Bibliography

1. http://www.ehornecker.de/TangiblesFramework.html

2. https://www.arduino.cc/en/Main/Products

3. https://www.google.com/url?sa=i&url=https%3A%2F%2Frandomnerdtutorials.com%2F21-arduino-modules-you-can-buy-for-less-than-2%2F&psig=AOvVaw3ybNAvPztcFf354zPepDlE&ust=1615797189513000&source=images&cd=vfe&ved=0CA0QjhxqFwoTCKDbnd6vr-8CFQAAAAAdAAAAABAF

4. https://www.youtube.com/watch?v=NePXqRwvmbs

CHAPTER 8

Interfaces for AI, Virtual Agents and Chatbots

Key learnings -

- ❖ Fundamentals of artificial intelligence-based interface design
- ❖ Strategies to design virtual agents and chatbots
- ❖ Case study on dialog design for chatbot

1. Definition of AI, Agents and Chatbots

According to IBM, any system capable of simulating human intelligence and thought processes is said to have "Artificial Intelligence" (AI). John McCarthy, together with Alan Turing, Marvin Minsky, Allen Newell, and Herbert A. Simon (A Nobel Prize winner in Design Economics in1978) are "founding fathers" of artificial intelligence. Hence, AI is the simulation of human like intelligence. The concept of AI came from anthropomorphism (provenance of humanness into nonhuman objects) in computers and robots. Virtual agents (artificial humans) are part of many AI based systems and they behave and communicate like human beings. Riya is very famous virtual agent probably the first used for communication purpose. Now users are familiar with many virtual agents like DISHA in IRCTC website, EVA in HDFC bank website, ILA in www.sbicard.com etc. Most of these virtual agents are coming with an AI based chatbots. Chatbots are nothing but the chat box enabled conversational AI for dialogs exchange with real users to a particular context.

Although the AI is a buzz word, the concepts of machine learning and deep learning approaches are important for AI based chatbot design and development. The machine learning (ML) is the study of computer algorithms that improve automatic through external inputs provided by users. Machine learning requires the development of algorithms (a mathematical model) based on training data (sample data), in order to make better predictions or decisions without being a rigidly programmed to do so.

Deep learning (also known as deep structured learning) is extended family of machine learning methods based on artificial neural networks with representation learning. For example, most of the speech recognition researchers are applying knowledge of deep learning after Defense Advanced Research Projects Agency (DARPA).

2. AI Design Framework

The Artificial Intelligence Board of America (ARtiBA) has proposed a multidisciplinary framework for designing AI solutions. According to this framework, for the desired AI results following questions may be answered –

- Why we need AI for humanity?
- Can we consider AI as a design challenge?

- Can we think a solution without a software?
- What is the strategy to influence other disciplines?
- How can we amalgamate insights from other disciplines for better cognitive outcomes?
- How can we rigorously comprehend the human-computer interface?

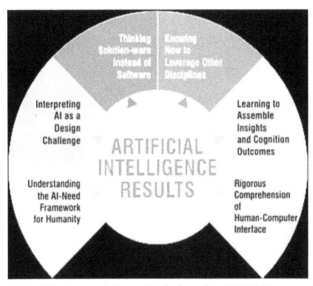

Fig. 8.1. The Design-Solution-Multidiscipline (DSM) Framework for AI Engineering Excellence (adapted from www.artiba.org).

Please remember, this framework is not only helping in agents and chatbots design but also applicable for designing other kinds of AI.

3. Narration and Dialogs Design for Chatbots and its application

Narrations and dialogs design are very important at initial part of chatbots design. This is an integral part of any conversational AI. Designers need to consider the AI as a human entity and need to prepare the AI bots with versatile responses against different queries raised by target users. Narratives between an AI chat bot for heart attack management (please see **Fig.8.2**) with users are as follows:

Chatbot: Hello! / I can help you to assess some irregular symptoms and figure out if you have any heart related health issues / Do you have any family history of heart attack?
Options: Yes / No/ I don't know
User: Yes

Chatbot: What is your gender?
Options: Male / Female
User: Male

Chatbot: Are you experiencing any of these symptoms?
Options: Chest pain in the left side radiating towards the left arm/ Indigestions/ Profuse Sweating/ Neck Pain /Chest Discomfort/ Shortness of Breath
User: Selected - Chest pain in the left side radiating towards the left arm + Profuse Sweating

Chatbot: Based on the assessment done, I think there might be possibility that you are experiencing a heart attack

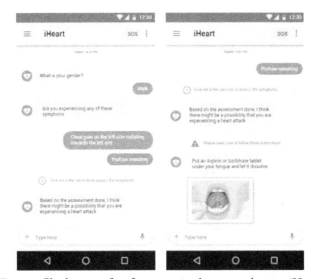

Fig. 8.2 Chatbot interface for managing heart attack using iHeart app.

4. Agents and Its Applications in web UI design

Suppose there is a commerce graduate who fears to see statistics module but wants to learn about variables and other statistics like student t test. He decided to learn about it from StatsGuru. StatsGuru is a virtual agent which helps with all queries related to statistic. The virtual agent asks some general questions to see how much knowledge does a student has. During the general Q and A session StatsGuru understands his level of user's knowledge and starts assisting accordingly. StatsGuru guides Sameer with how to find out variables. He also provides the student with a video link which has examples for variables to make it clearer about the topic. StatsGuru ask him does he has any other questions. The student was happy and enlighten with the knowledge and thank StatsGuru for helping out.

Fig. 8.3 Virtual agent-based Interface of StatGuru.

Bibliography

1. https://www.artiba.org/the-artiba-edge#:~
:text=AI%20Design%20%26%20Engineering%20
Excellence%20%E2%80%93%20The%20
ARTIBA%20Solution&text=The%20
AMDEX%E2%84%A2%20framework%20
is,70%20companies%20across%209%20countries

CHAPTER 9

Fundamentals of System Design and Programing Languages for UX and Interaction Designers

Key learnings -

❖ Concept of system design
❖ Product service system
❖ Software Processes and Interactions
❖ Basics and application of programming languages

1. **System Design Approaches and Architecting Software**

Understanding of system design is very important when providing end-to-end solutions to a set of problems. A system is a concept where different entities or stakeholders (as a part of a system) are interacting between each other in a process to get a desired outcome, considering the surrounding environment.

Now-a-days, product service system (PSS) is very crucial as many products are depending on time-to-time service requirements. For instances, the Aqua guard water purifier requires to change the filter cartridge every six months, Amazon provides e-commerce platform along with logistic services to product retailers etc. Further, most of the product allied services are now software mediated. Therefore, there are numerous opportunities for designing the software-based PSS. In this context it is reasonable to mention that there are many ways to conceptualize the system and representation of system concept. However, the system representation using UML diagrams is a formal way of presentation.

2. UML diagrams in system design

Unified modeling language (UML) diagrams are very useful for representation of concepts of dynamic systems. Structural modeling (SM) is possible using UML diagrams. The SM captures the static features of a system. On the other side, behavioral model (BM) describes the interaction in the system. There are three major diagrams useful for visualizing system from BM point of views. These are –

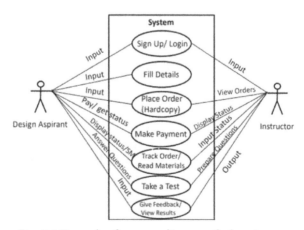

Fig. 9.1 Example of use case diagram of e-learning system.

- *Use case Diagram:* These diagrams are a set of use cases, actors, and their relationships (see **Fig. 9.1**). They represent the use case view of a system. A use case represents a particular functionality of a system. Hence, use case diagram is used to describe the relationships among the functionalities and their internal/external controllers. These controllers are known as actors.

- *Activity Diagram:* It is to explore the logic of a complex operation / a complex business rule/ a single use case/ several use cases / a business process/ software processes) is useful for showing workflow and parallel processing (see **Fig. 9.2**).

- *Sequence Diagram:* It is an interaction diagram. From the name, it is clear that the diagram deals with some sequences, which are the sequence of messages flowing from one object to another. Interaction among the components of a system is very important from implementation and execution perspective. Sequence diagram is used to visualize the sequence of calls in a system to perform a specific functionality (see **Fig. 9.3**).

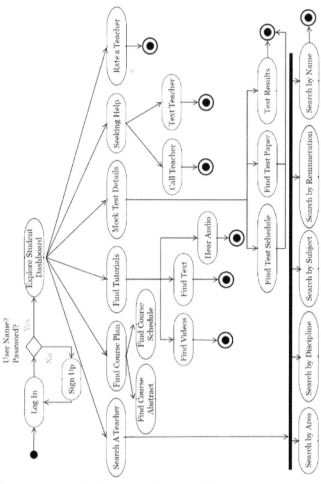

Fig. 9.2 Example of activity diagram of learning management system.

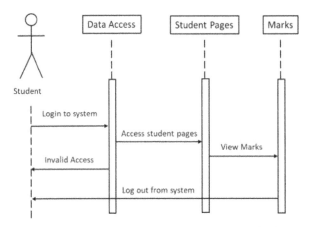

Fig. 9.3 Example of sequence diagram of a part of a learning management system.

3. Programming Languages and its Importance in UI Design

It is good to know the type of languages software developers are using for the websites and app development.

3.1. HTML

The hypertext markup language (HTML) is a programming language, very useful for UI development of a website. This language helps to describe the structure of the webpage. The HTML is consisting of a series of elements that instruct the browser the way to display the content. The following is the basic structure of HTML:

```
<!DOCTYPE html>
<html>
<head>
<title> Title of the Page </title>
</head>
<body>
<h1>Our First Heading (heading 1) </h1>
<p> Our first paragraph (paragraph 1) </p>
</body>
</html>
```

The text highlighted as bold in the above programme should be displayed on the browser.

3.2. JavaScript

JavaScript (JS) helps to program the behavior of web pages and its comparatively easier language to learn. The application of JS is not limited to Web pages, many desktop and server programs use JS. Node.js is the best known. Some other databases, such as MongoDB and CouchDB, also use JavaScript as a programming language. Following is the most frequently use example of getting element by ID:

```
document.getElementById("demo").innerHTML =
"Hello JavaScript";
```

3.3. CSS

Cascading Styling Sheets (CSS) is very important when a developer is trying to show some dynamic content/ element on the website. The CSS describes the way the HTML elements are to be displayed on screen, paper, or in other media. The CSS can control the layout of multiple web pages, consistently all at once. The basic structure of the CSS has been presented as follows:

```
body {
  background-color: lightblue;
}

h1 {
  color: white;
  text-align: center;
}

p {
  font-family: verdana;
  font-size: 20px;
}
```

In CSS, it is possible to define background colour, font colour, font family, font size, alignment etc. in a webpage. However, the react / bootstrap-modal are responsive framework that are comparatively easier way to generate codes for websites. The API and syntaxes for modal is also available online. Bootstrap is the most popular HTML, CSS, and JavaScript framework for developing responsive, mobile-first websites.

3.4. XML

The eXtensible Markup Language (XML) is a programming language which is very similar to HTML. The XML is designed to store and transport data in a self-descriptive manner. This language is applicable for mobile app interface design. Following is the example of a basic XML programme for sending a message from Sham to Ram:

```
<note>
  <to>Ram</to>
  <from>Shyam</from>
  <heading>Reminder</heading>
  <body>Meet me this weekend! </body>
</note>
```

3.5. Java

Java is an object-oriented programming language. Java is used to develop specially the mobile apps, but also web apps, desktop apps, games and much more.

This programming language works on different platforms such as Windows, Mac, Linux, Raspberry Pi, etc. It is easy to learn and simple to use and open-source and free

Like C++, Java also allows code to be reused, lowering development costs. A basic Java structure is presented as follows:

```
public class MyClass {
  public static void main(String[] args) {
    System.out.println("Hello World");
  }
}
```

3.6. SQL

The Structured Query Language (SQL) is a standard language for storing, manipulating and retrieving data in databases. The SQL can do the following:

- execute queries against a database
- retrieve data from a database
- insert records in a database
- update records in a database
- delete records from a database
- create new databases
- create new tables in a database
- create stored procedures in a database
- create views in a database
- set permissions on tables, procedures, and views

These are many SQLs; MySQL is very common among these. Syntaxes for minimum and maximum are presented as follows:

```
SELECT MIN(column_name)
FROM table_name
WHERE condition;

SELECT MAX(column_name)
FROM table_name
WHERE condition;
```

3.7. PHP

The PHP (Hypertext Preprocessor) widely-used for, open source scripting language, are generally executed on the server. The PHP can be applied for –

- generating dynamic page content
- creating, opening, reading, writing, deleting, and closing files on the server
- collecting form data

- sending and receiving cookies
- adding, deleting, modifying data in the crated database
- controlling user-access
- encrypting data

The basic structure of a PHP programme is as follows:

```
<!DOCTYPE html>
<html>
<body>

<?php
echo "I have encoded my first PHP script!";
?>

</body>
</html>
```

It is possible to apply this language for e-commerce website development.

3.8. C/ C++

The C++ is an object-oriented popular programming language generally used to create computer programs. This programming language is found in many operating systems, Graphical User Interfaces, and embedded systems. In C++, a clear structure to programs has been given and it allows code to be reused, lowering development costs.

The C++ is a transferable and it might be used to develop applications i.e. adapted to multiple platforms.

```
int main() {
  cout << "Hello World!";
  return 0;
}
```

In this context, it would be reasonable to mention that learning of C++ is also useful for Arduino and sensor based tangible and IoT interface design.

3.9. Python

In 1991, Guido van Rossum released the Python which is now very popular programming language. The Python could be used for:

- statistics and mathematics
- software development
- dynamic website development (server-side)
- system scripting

It is possible to run the following Pyton programme, by opening the command line, navigate to the directory where the Python file (python helloworld.py) saved in a computer file:

PROGRAMME:
print("Hello, World!")

INPUT in COMMAND LINE:
C:\Users\Your Name>python helloworld.py

OUTPUT:
Hello, World!

3.10. R & R studio

The R is a programming language along with a software environment that is beneficial for statistical analysis, data modeling, graphical representation, data mining and reporting.

Both the descriptive (e.g. mean, mode, median etc.) and inferential statistics (e.g. Chi-square tests, Student t-tests etc.) can be computed in the R.

Bibliography

1. https://www.w3schools.com/html/default.asp
2. https://react-bootstrap.github.io/components/modal/

***

CHAPTER 10

Design Ethics and Intellectual Property Rights

Key learnings -

❖ An overview on design ethics
❖ Importance of intellectual property right (IPR)
❖ Types and definitions of different IPRs including design registration, patents, trademark, copyright etc.
❖ Possibilities and cases of IPR registrations

1. **Design Ethics (Copy the concept and change the visual design/ Animal forms for dustbins)**

Design ethics is the discussion of legal and ethical grounds related to design to various design contexts. The study of design ethics helps designers to understand the legal matters related to design. Design integrity could be retained by study of design ethics. It focuses on –

- *Design policies*: Design solutions should not violet design policy of the country
- *Legal matters*: Designers should not copy or still others' work or design
- *Intellectual properties*: Registration of design is important before publishing or popularizing the design solution to claim the own design.
- *Human ethics*: Human involvement in design process is profound now-a-days. Designers should not force any target users to give a favorable feedback for the design solutions.
- *Animal ethics*: Designers should consider animal ethics when designing anything related to wildlife.
- *Social and Cultural policies*: The designer should respect the social integrity and cultural values when providing design solutions.
- Environmental Policies: Designers should be aware of environmental conditions and policies while designing products or systems and utilize environment friendly resources.
- Etc.

Many times, designers create artificial crisis (manmade) in the product market to sale highly innovative features like iPhone. However, designers need to think about design ethics when creating artificial crisis in the market. In this context, surprisingly, it was observed that many retailers have been started to sale 3 wheels cabin mobility scooters in the COVID-19 scenario. Now the question might arise in mind–

Is there any possibility to violate the design ethics for creating artificial needs in market to sale such product?

2. IPR registration in India and Abroad

The intellectual property right (IPR) is very important for business and innovation purpose. Designers, design researchers and design academicians, all can innovate and go for IPR registration in India and Abroad. Please remember IPR registration id country specific, which means if an innovator registered with the IPR in India but not for other countries, business can be continued on same innovation without permission at the other country. Therefore, to secure the innovation across the globe, multiple IPR registrations are required for multiple countries. Therefore, it is very important to have IPR registration from the business perspective. There are various kinds of IPR possible to register in India. These are –

- Design Registration
- Copyright Registration
- Trademark (TM) Registration
- Patent Registration
- Geographical Indication (GI) Registry

3. Design Registration

Design registration can be done when the industrial designer creates new and original features of novel shape, configuration, surface pattern, ornamentations and composition of lines or colours applied to articles or products which in turn appeal consumers and are judged solely by the eye. Therefore, significant and unique aesthetic changes in the existing product or the unique visual change that makes a new product, can be considered for design registration.

4. Copyright Registration

The objective of copyright registration is to record a verifiable account of the *date and content of the work*, so that a legal claim, or case of infringement or plagiarism can be made by the copyright owner. The copyright owner can also produce a copy of the work from an official government source.

5. Trademark

A trademark is a visual sign or symbol or logo which might include a word, name, label or numeral used by a business to distinguish its goods or services from other similar products or services in the market owned by other businesses.

6. Patent

A novel process or mechanism or technology for product can be registered under the patent act of Government of India. Novel processes might be involved in design of a software, robots, complex machine, fermentation process, any other chemical process etc. can be considered for patents.

7. GI Registry

A geographical indication (GI) is a name or sign used on certain products which corresponds to a specific geographical location or origin (e.g., a town, region, or country). A business community or social community-based organization who are selling product of specialty of a region can go for GI registration in India. For instances, Rasgulla is registered as GI from Kolkata, West Bengal, India.

Bibliography

1. http://www.ipindia.nic.in/
2. http://copyright.gov.in/

———————— *** ————————

APPENDIX

Useful Templets for UX and UI Designers

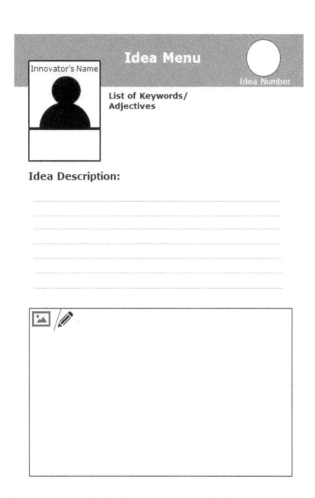

Idea Menu

Innovator's Name

Idea Number

List of Keywords/ Adjectives

Idea Description:

*Idea menu is useful for brainstorming and ideation process.

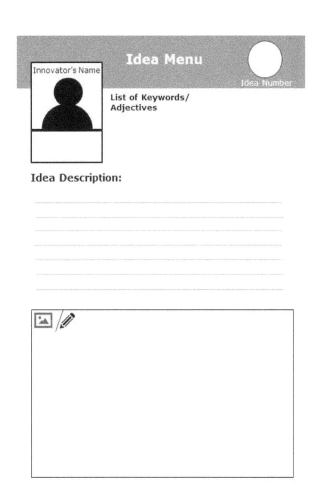

*Idea menu is useful for brainstorming and ideation process.

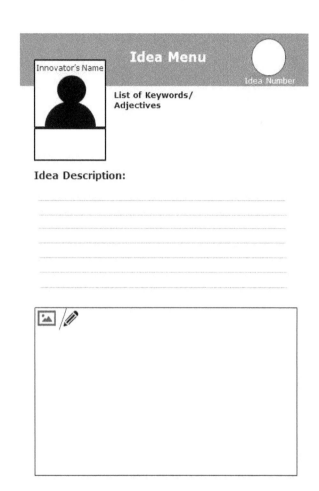

*Idea menu is useful for brainstorming and ideation process.

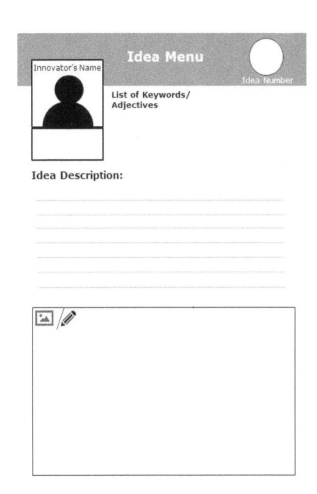

Idea Description:

*Idea menu is useful for brainstorming and ideation process.

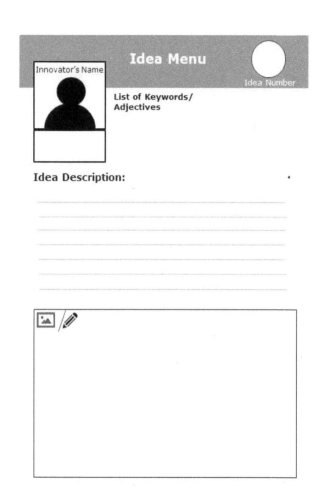

*Idea menu is useful for brainstorming and ideation process.

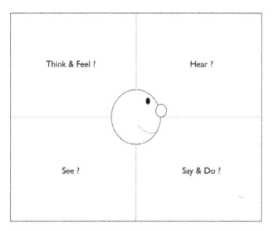

Think & Feel ?   Hear ?

See ?   Say & Do ?

*Empathy map template is useful for empathizing
with users and understanding user feelings

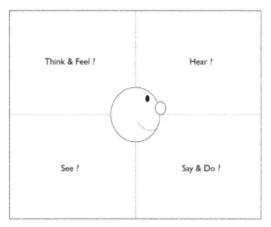

Think & Feel ?

Hear ?

See ?

Say & Do ?

*Empathy map template is useful for empathizing
with users and understanding user feelings

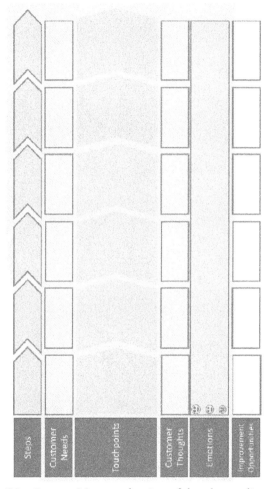

Steps | Customer Needs | Touch-points | Customer Thoughts | Emotions | Improvement Opportunities

*User Journey Map template is useful understanding different touchpoints along with process and user emotions

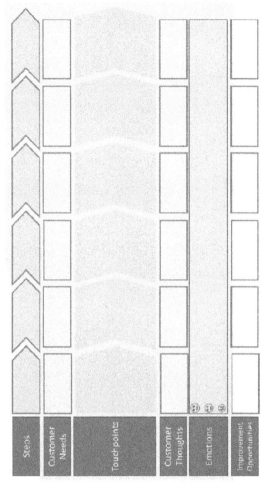

*User Journey Map template is useful understanding
different touchpoints along with process and user emotions

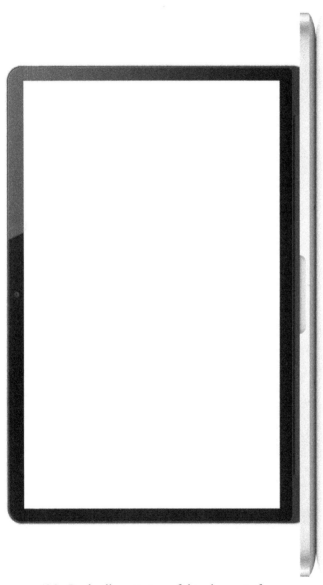

*MacBook silhouette is useful to draw wireframes.

*MacBook silhouette is useful to draw wireframes.

*MacBook silhouette is useful to draw wireframes.

*MacBook silhouette is useful to draw wireframes.

*MacBook silhouette is useful to draw wireframes.

*i-Phone silhouette is useful to draw wireframes.

*i-Phone silhouette is useful to draw wireframes.

*i-Phone silhouette is useful to draw wireframes.

*i-Phone silhouette is useful to draw wireframes.

*i-Phone silhouette is useful to draw wireframes.

UX Notes